THE FAITH DIFFERENCE

Prayers, Lessons, Activities,
and Games for Teens

THE FAITH DIFFERENCE

KIERAN SAWYER, S.S.N.D.

ave maria press   Notre Dame, Indiana

Imprimatur: The Most Reverend Rembert. G. Weakland, O.S.B., D.D.
Archbishop of Milwaukee
Given at Milwaukee, WI on 21 November 2000.

The *Imprimatur* is an official declaration that a book is free of doctrinal or moral error. No implication is contained therein that those who have granted the *Imprimatur* endorse its contents, opinions, or statements expressed.

Some of the materials in this book originally appeared in *The Jesus Difference* (1987) and *The Risk of Faith* (1988) by Kieran Sawyer, SSND. Both books were published by Ave Maria Press.

Founded in 1865, Ave Maria Press is a ministry of the Indiana Province of Holy Cross.

www.avemariapress.com

ISBN-10 0-87793-729-X   ISBN-13 978-0-87793-729-6

Cover and text design by Katherine Robinson Coleman

Printed and bound in the United States of America.

Contents

Introduction

The presentations, exercises, prayers, and games in this book have been used for more than thirty years with thousands of teens in hundreds of different settings and formats. Originally developed for use at the TYME OUT Youth Center in the Milwaukee area, these materials were first published by Ave Maria Press in two separate books, *The Jesus Difference* and *The Risk of Faith*. Since the books went out of print, I have heard from many youth ministers, catechists, and religion teachers who continue to tell me how well these materials work with their youth—and how worn their old books have become after years of use!

Now, in *The Faith Difference* I have re-gathered all of the best materials from those two books and reorganized them into five easy-to-use sections for use with senior high school teens: presentations and responses, community building, discussions and exercises, prayers, and games. The activities found in *The Faith Difference* can be used for retreats in a variety of timeframes and in a variety of other youth sessions. These include:

Weekend retreats A two-night overnight is an ideal time span for a youth retreat. A weekend offers time to provide a concentrated faith experience that incorporates most of the elements of total youth ministry—a deepening of prayer, an increased sense of belonging in the community of faith, interaction with adult Christians and with other youth, and informal celebrations of reconciliation and Eucharist.

One-night retreats A one-night retreat offers most of the advantages of the weekend retreat. You will often find, however, that it is time to leave just about when the group is getting into the spirit. I recommend one-night retreats for younger teenagers.

One-day retreats I find one-day retreats to be less than ideal, especially if they are held during school hours. The young people seem to have difficulty entering into the retreat spirit in so short a time. However, if you have only seven or eight hours to spend with your group, the magic hours from 4 p.m. to midnight are much better than daytime hours. Rather than schedule a day of reflection on the young people's free day, hold it in the afternoon and evening before the free day and let them have their entire day off to sleep.

Mini-retreats and "twilights" Late afternoon and evening sessions of three to five hours can also be very effective for youth activities. I find it difficult to accomplish anything with teenagers in less than three hours. That length of time is essential if you are to create a sense of community, hold a good discussion, develop an atmosphere for prayer, and have some fun.

Parent-youth evenings A mini-retreat with a group of young people and their parents can be a powerful communication builder as well as a faith-filled experience for both age groups. I usually set up the dialogue groups so that the teenagers are not in the same group with their parents. They seem to be able to relate on an adult level with other parents more easily than with their own.

Confirmation preparation sessions Many groups preparing for the sacrament of confirmation try to develop a deep bond between candidates and also between the youth and their adult leaders. Many of these activities work well in confirmation sessions, especially when these sessions are held in at least 90 minute segments.

Youth group meetings Many of the themes and activities presented here, including several having to do with scripture, are most appropriate for regularly scheduled youth group or other parish youth sessions.

Religion classes Whereas for the most part religion classes taking place in a Catholic high school are purely academic in structure, there is always room for more affective learning situations and occasions of faith development for the students. Often the activities in *The Faith Difference* can reinforce and concretize material that is being covered as part of the regular curriculum.

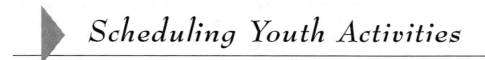

Scheduling Youth Activities

A facility away from the parish or school is preferred for many youth sessions, especially longer experiences like retreats. Finding a place for a retreat experience can be problematic. It is usually necessary to schedule the facility long in advance, as much as six months or a year. Take care in scheduling religious activities to avoid conflict with important school events like homecoming, prom, and major athletic tournaments. Young people should not be forced to choose between the retreat and these other events.

Settings

The activities in *The Faith Difference* use a variety of settings. In an ideal situation the following kinds of spaces would be available. Of course, you will have to adapt to the space you have at hand.

Large group presentation space An area where the entire group can be seated on beanbag chairs, floor cushions, or chairs close to the leader and the chalkboard.

Discussion tables A space where the participants can meet in groups of six to eight, preferably around square or round tables. Long narrow cafeteria type tables do not work for discussion groups. If small tables are not available, form the discussion groups without tables.

Cozy corners Comfortable settings where each of the small groups can gather. Couches, beanbags, or floor cushions are helpful.

Prayer space A comfortable area, preferably carpeted, large enough so the group can sit on the floor in a circle. It may be possible to use the church sanctuary for these activities.

"Alone" spots A space large enough for the participants to spread out for quiet times of individual prayer and reflection (but within the voice and eye range of the leader). The church, gym, or cafeteria can often be used for this. A supply of cushions or carpet pieces is helpful.

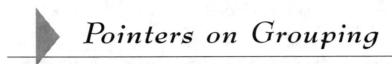

Pointers on Grouping

The activities can be conducted with any size group provided there is adult participation, adequate space, and a good sound system. An ideal size is 30 to 40 participants, including the adults, broken down into groups of seven or eight. If there are more than 50 youth, it may be desirable to split the group and meet at two different times. One advantage of the split group is that it gives the teenagers two dates to choose from and so cuts down on absenteeism.

You will need some fast, efficient ways of dividing the participants into dialogue groups. The composition of these groups is important for the success of each session. Each group should contain an even distribution of adult leaders, youth leaders, boys, girls, outspoken and shy individuals, and so on. Try to separate members of friendship groups and always separate family members. For most activities it is better not to allow participants to select their own groups.

Some grouping methods are given on pages 155-156.

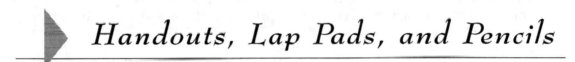

Handouts, Lap Pads, and Pencils

Many of the activities are accompanied by a handout sheet. The handouts are meant to be discussion and reflection guides and should never be used simply as worksheets. Detailed directions on how to use each handout are given in the text. If the activities are to be used on a retreat, it is wise to supply each student with a folder in which to keep the collection of handouts received on the retreat.

Procure a set of heavy cardboard pieces about 8" x 10" to use as lap pads whenever there is an activity away from tables that requires writing.

Pens or pencils are necessary for most activities that involve handouts.

Adult Involvement

The activities in *The Faith Difference* require active adult participation, ideally one adult for every six to eight teenagers. However, except for the person (or team) who directs the sessions, these adults do not have to put in preparation time. They are present simply as participants, doing whatever the young people do. Their primary purpose is to represent the adult Christian community whose living faith is being shared with the young people. Their presence in the youth activities is essential if the young people are to develop a real sense of belonging in the church.

Several levels of adult involvement are needed:

The Coordinator This person (for example, the Director of Religious Education or Director of Youth Ministry) organizes the youth gathering, chooses the theme or topic, recruits the catechist(s), sets the date, invites the youth participants, recruits the adult and youth leaders, schedules the place, and arranges the setting, food, transportation, liturgists, music, and so on.

The Catechist(s) This person (or team) studies the activities selected, prepares the content, gathers the needed materials, presents the input sessions, and facilitates the group activities, prayer experiences, and games. It is helpful if the catechist has teaching experience or has worked with groups of teens in some other capacity.

The Group Leaders These volunteer adults and older youth participate in all of the group activities. They act as small-group leaders and help with the chaperoning of the group. In overnight retreats they are responsible for the supervision of the dormitories. We recommend one adult group leader for every six or seven teenagers. In an ideal situation every small group has a youth leader in addition. Youth leaders should be two or more years older than the retreat group or class.

Others Involving many members of the total community—parents, relatives, friends, neighbors, and parishioners—in the youth sessions helps to develop in the teens a sense of belonging in their parish or school. Members of the parish or school family can be invited to:

- pray for the young people enrolled in the class or attending the program, retreat, or rally

- send letters of encouragement to the teens

- provide meals or snacks

- provide sleeping space and breakfast for small groups (six to eight) when no retreat center is available

- provide transportation

- help pay program fees

- gather for send-off or welcome-home ceremonies

- attend the closing liturgy

▶ Dialogue: Why and How

The activities in *The Faith Difference* depend for their effectiveness on the interaction of the participants—the interaction of youth with adults, and of youth with youth. This interaction is brought about primarily through dialogue. Some of the dialogue is light, fun, and humorous. Its purpose is to break down barriers and to build mutual understanding and enjoyment. It also makes serious dialogue possible. Serious dialogue, the heart of all of these activities, helps the participants to share with one another their dreams and hopes, their questions and doubts, their values and goals, their faith and prayer.

The dialogue process is based on several assumptions:

▶ that faith is already present in each person, and that dialogue helps to surface, affirm, and strengthen that faith;

▶ that each person is a source of truth and wisdom, and that the truth of each individual is meant for and needed by the entire community;

▶ that all people, especially youth, want to open their hearts and share their deepest beliefs and doubts; all they need is listeners who care;

▶ that talking about the deepest values in a person's life helps to clarify and strengthen them for the speaker; a person understands better what he or she has tried to articulate to another;

▶ that the faith of the listener is also strengthened by the dialogue process; one of the most effective ways of alerting a person to the action of God in his or her own life is to hear about God's action in the life of another;

▶ that dialogue creates common meanings and values that enable those who participate in it to become a community of faith.

Dialogue of the sort described here can happen only in an atmosphere of openness and trust. To establish such an atmosphere is to a large extent the responsibility of the catechist. But it also true that dialogue itself can create such an atmosphere. Young people learn to share deeply with one another and with adults by dialoguing. The catechist's role is to make it easy.

The dialogue activities in *The Faith Difference* are designed to encourage sharing. Though each activity uses a slightly different dialogue technique, some general methodological principles apply:

Pre-response Everyone is given a chance to record his or her response in some way before being asked to respond orally. The pre-response might be written, shown with hand signals, or indicated by body positions. The responding is made easy by asking a very specific question with a definite answer, by providing sentence starters, or by giving a spread of answers to choose from. These techniques get everyone involved in thinking about the question, make it clear that there is a spread of opinion on the answer rather than one "right" response, and create the need for an individual to examine a position that is contrary to other positions presented.

Dialogue starters Getting started with the dialogue is facilitated by designating the first speaker, often in a humorous way; for example, the person with the curliest hair, the person with the next birthday, the person wearing the most faded jeans. Each person then takes a turn around the circle. The starter designation usually creates a little burst of laughter and further relaxes the group.

Pass option The sharing must always be done freely. If at any time a participant is asked a question he or she doesn't know how to answer, or doesn't want to answer in public, the person simply says "Pass." The pass option is, I believe, the single most effective technique in creating an atmosphere where open dialogue can happen. Given the choice of either answering honestly or passing, young people almost always choose to answer. But the pass option is always there as a safe and easy way out if they are threatened by the question in any way. It is imperative that the pass option be respected by the catechist and by all the participants.

Gradual deepening The dialogue moves gradually from light, easy topics to more serious ones. The easier sharing both teaches the technique and warms the participants to one another, thus facilitating the deeper sharing.

Listening Listening is essential to the dialogue process. Everyone in the dialogue circle shares in the listening role. It is important for all the members of the group to look at the speaker, to respond facially to what is being said, and to ask follow-up questions. The adults should be especially present to each speaker; at the same time, the adults will need to be careful not to become the focus toward which all comments or answers are directed.

 *Discipline*

An important component in any activity with adolescents is discipline. The participants are young adults in many ways and children in many others. Youth leaders vary widely in the kind of conduct that they expect from teenagers and in the disciplinary methods they use with them. I find that the best discipline for youth activities is a well-planned schedule with definite activities that are both enjoyable and involving, and a limited amount of free time.

I also believe in rules—"preventive discipline." I present an explicit code of conduct, explaining the reason behind each rule, and I simply expect the young people I work with to comply. More often than not, they respect this expectation.

A sample copy of the rules we use at TYME OUT is found on pages 157. This may help you in creating a set of rules which fit your circumstances and the leadership style of your team.

PRESENTATIONS
&
RESPONSES

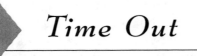

Time Out

Most young people have not had much experience with retreats. This short opening session compares a retreat to the time out in a sporting game. The session sets the tone for the retreat and helps the young people to understand what they can expect in the hours ahead.

Materials and Preparations Needed:

▶ cushions or pillows arranged in an informal circle

▶ a recording of a song with lyrics that speak to this theme (e.g., making time for God, taking time out from the business of life)

▶ a candle

Directions:

1. Invite the participants to join you in the prayer circle. Dim the lights, place the candle in the circle, pass out the words of the song (if you have them), and give a short talk based on the following script.

Script

A retreat is like the time out in a game of basketball or football. The whistle blows, the game stops, and the coach gathers the team in a huddle. The coach and the team take time to check out their game plan, to evaluate how they are playing, and to try to figure out some new strategies for winning. The time out is important for individual players as well as for the team. It's an opportunity to see if each person is playing the best game possible and if the team is working together to accomplish its common goal.

A retreat is a "time out" in the game of life. In a sense, "the game" has stopped for a short period of time. None of you is doing what you usually do on a Friday night. We've stopped the game so you can take time to examine how well you're playing it. What new moves do you need in order to play the game better? What bad habits do you have to start paying attention to? Whose game plan are you following? How serious is your desire to play well?

During this time out you'll be spending time conferring with your teammates, sharing with them your perspectives on the game, your successes and hopes, your fears and frustrations. You'll also have a chance to dialogue with the adult leaders. They have been playing this game called life for a lot of years; you can probably learn much from their successes and failures.

But the most important reason for the time out is so that we can all spend some time listening to the head coach, God. He's the one, after all, who has mapped out the game plan for us. God has us all in this big huddle and has his arms around all of our shoulders. We, your retreat leaders, are like God's assistant coaches. Our job is to help you hear what the head coach is saying and to pass his directions on to you. We ask that you be praying for us during this retreat; pray that we keep our hearts open to whatever God wants to say to you through us.

Whether this time out makes a difference in your personal game plan or not is up to you. If you are open and positive and cooperative, then I can guarantee that the retreat will be a wonderful experience for you. It might even be one of the most valuable weekends of your life.

It's possible, however, for a person to waste a retreat. Some people come on retreat with closed minds. They're not willing or able to allow God or anyone else to get inside their hearts. Some people may be angry or upset about something going on back home. Others come on retreat just to fool around and have fun. For some reason, maybe immaturity, they're not ready to do any serious thinking and praying about their lives. Sometimes young people cop out on retreat by using alcohol or other drugs. They choose this method of avoiding the deep thinking about life that the retreat requires. Another way to waste the time is to get too little sleep. Like any game, the game of life requires discipline and training, and a good night's sleep is a must for top performance.

Let's spend some time now in quiet prayer, trying to get in touch with the God who lives in each of our hearts. To help us get in the mood for prayer, I'm going to play a song that (e.g., speaks about the need to take some time out in our busy lives to spend time with God). Listen to the song prayerfully and hear God asking you to give him the time of this retreat *(adapt this part to fit the song you have chosen).*

2.   After the song is finished, say:

Now talk to God quietly in your own heart. Tell him how you feel about giving him the time of this retreat. If you're afraid, tell him so. If you're glad you came, tell him that. If you're feeling angry and negative, tell him that, too, and ask him to help you to be more positive and open. *(Allow time.)* Ask God, now, to bless your teammates in the game of life: your family members, your friends, your school companions. Mention by name each of the special people in your life and ask God to be with them this weekend wherever they are. Pray especially for the friends who are here on the retreat with you. Pray that this weekend will be "good" time for all of you.

▶ *On the Edge of an Adventure**

This presentation helps young people look upon faith as an adventure and examine their openness to the challenges faith offers them. The activities were designed for use early in a retreat but can be easily adapted for use in other settings. The activities work very well with groups that are completing preparation for confirmation. Substitute "confirmation program" for "youth program" when applicable.

Materials and Preparations Needed:

▶ copies of the "Beginnings" (page 21), "On the Edge of an Adventure" (page 22), and "Adventures in Faith" (page 23) handouts for each participant

Directions:

1. Give out copies of the "Beginnings" handout and say:

   Let's begin with No. 1 on the handout. Circle the letter that indicates best how you usually respond when faced with a new situation.

2. Read the question and the answers aloud, then say:

   If none of these answers fits, write your own at letter i.

3. Allow time. Then read No. 2 in the same way. Allow time for those responses as well. Say:

   Now look at No. 3. If you *knew* you would not fall on your face, what great adventure would you like to try in the very near future? You might pick an action-packed adventure like sky-diving or shooting the rapids in a canoe. Or you might choose an accomplishment type of adventure like singing solo for the music festival or running for class president. Or your adventure might be in the area of relationships, perhaps having a heart-to-heart conversation with your dad or talking to a certain girl or guy.

4. Allow time for everyone to finish the sentence. Then, say:

   Now share your answers to these three questions with your small group. Go around the circle once with each person telling how he or she completed the sentence in No. 3. Then go around a second time and explain the responses to Nos. 1 and 2. Talk about the answers; explain *why* you circled the letter you did. The first speaker will be the person with the most adventurous hair style.

* I am indebted to Lyman Coleman and the *Serendipity Series* for some of the ideas in this session. For a list of Coleman's publications both in and out of print see www.amazon.com.

5. For the next part of the presentation, a "scripture adventure," have the participants sit at dialogue tables, but ask them to turn their chairs so they are facing you. Then, say:

> When we read the gospels, or hear them read, we often fail to realize that the events there involve ordinary people like us, people who don't understand what is happening to them. For the apostles, knowing Jesus and spending time with him was a daily adventure. They never quite knew what would happen next.
>
> I'm going to read a passage from Matthew's gospel. As I read, try to get inside the story. Imagine what it would have been like to be there, to be one of the disciples in that boat. The gospel story begins right after the multiplication of the loaves. As followers of Jesus, we have just helped him distribute five loaves of bread and two fishes to five thousand people. Jesus has dismissed the crowd and we are all resting on the hillside, still mystified at all we have seen and heard today.

6. Read the story from the "On the Edge of an Adventure" handout dramatically. Try to emphasize what it would have been like to participate in the events you are narrating. After the reading pass out the handout and say:

> If you had been Peter, how do you think you would have reacted to Jesus' invitation to walk on water? Remember, it's the middle of a dark night, the waves are washing over the boat, and you aren't sure if the figure on the water is Jesus or a ghost. Raise your hand if you would have shrunk back in terror . . . asked someone else to go first . . . (continue reading the possible answers to question one of the handout).

7. This next section is the core of this exercise. Prepare it well so that it becomes an in-depth talk on faith rather than a fill-in-the-blanks exercise. Be sure everyone is looking at you so that you can make eye contact as you talk. Expand on each of the faith stances explained in letters **a** through **g** below, adding examples from your own life and the lives of young people you know. Say:

> We're going to use the scripture story now to help us think about our own relationship with God. Which part of the story best describes what is going on in your heart right now?
>
> **a.** Some of you may be like Jesus at the beginning of the story. You've had it with people and work. You need time to get away, time to think, time to pray, time to get your mind and heart straightened out. If that description fits you, circle the letter *a* under question two.
>
> **b.** Some of you may be at a stage in your life where your faith is sure. You know God is present in you and with you. You can almost hear him saying, "I'm here. Don't be afraid. I'll take care of things for you." If trust in God's presence and loving care is strong in your life right now, circle the letter *b*.
>
> **c.** Some of you, on the other hand, might be like the disciples in the story who think they are seeing a ghost, not Jesus. People *tell* you about God, sometimes you even think you catch a glimpse of him, but you aren't sure

if he really exists. Maybe, you think, God is just a figment of people's imaginations. If this is a doubting period in your life, circle the letter *c*.

d. Maybe some of you are like Peter in the story: You want a sign. If God is in your life, you'd like him to work a miracle or two just for you. "Lord, if it's really you," you say, "get me that job I need, or make my mom stop drinking, or help me make the varsity team." If you're looking for a personal miracle to bolster your faith, circle the letter *d*.

e. Some of you may find that you are coming into a whole new awareness of God and what he wants of you. You find yourself being interested in religion and faith like you never were before. You want to get to know God better. You hear him inviting you to be more faithful to him and to the service of his people. It appears as a real possibility that Jesus might be inviting you to step out of your comfortable boat and do something special for him. If you sense in your heart a mysterious call to a deeper faith and service, circle the letter *e*.

f. Some of you may be up to your necks in trouble at this time in your life. You may feel as if you're drowning in a sea of problems—problems with your parents, problems with alcohol or drugs, problems with your friendship or love relationships, problems in school. Right now your relationship with God is one loud cry for help. "Save me, Lord, I'm going under!" Circle the letter *f* if I've just described your life.

g. And some of you might be like the disciples after the storm has passed. You *were* in trouble, you cried out to God for help, and he answered your prayers. His action in your life has truly strengthened your faith. If your heart knows by experience that Jesus has the power to calm the storms of life, circle the letter *g*.

8. Continue. Say:

Please, spend a few more minutes quietly thinking about where your heart is in relationship to God right now. Do you need time to find him? Do you trust his presence? Do you doubt that he even exists? Are you looking for a sign? hearing his invitation? crying for help? Are you deeply believing?

9. Allow a few minutes for quiet reflection. Then, say:

Please share your reflections on this question with your group. Begin with the group leader and go around the circle telling which letter or letters you circled and what the answers mean in your spiritual life. Remember, you are always free to pass if you do not want to share your response to a particular question.

10. Continue in small groups, though you may wish to have the participants move to less formal discussion circles. Give out the "Adventures in Faith" handout and say:

The first question here concerns your openness to this retreat. Grade your openness on the scale from 1 to 5. On the 1 end of the scale would be the people who are closed to the whole retreat idea. They really don't want to be here and they're not going to open up if they can help it. They're sitting tight in the boat. On the 5 end of the scale are people who are very open to the retreat. They are ready and willing to listen, to share, to pray, to have fun, to participate in any way they can. They've jumped into the water with both feet.

11. Allow time. Then say:

In the second question, circle the words that best describe how you feel about the possibility of really getting close to Jesus during this retreat.

12. Allow time. Continue:

This retreat is only one part of your youth program (or campus ministry). I'd like you to spend the next few minutes evaluating your entire program. Circle the letter in No. 3 that describes how you felt about the program (ministry) at the beginning. Box the letter that tells how you feel about it now.

13. Allow time for marking the question, then say:

Now share with your group your responses to these questions. On the first round talk about questions 1 and 2, your openness to the retreat, and your feelings about being invited by Jesus to come closer to him. On the second round, share your feelings about the youth program in your parish.

Behold, I make all things new . . .

YES, even you!

Beginnings

1. When it comes to doing something new, I am usually: (circle all that fit)

   a. just plain scared
   b. daring
   c. very careful
   d. afraid of failing
   e. afraid people will laugh at me
   f. a follower
   g. a leader
   h. willing to try anything
   i.

2. The thing I usually have to deal with before launching out on a new adventure is:

   a. lack of confidence in myself
   b. lack of faith in God
   c. fear of standing all alone
   d. fear of making a mistake
   e. indecision
   f. the impulse to rush in without sufficient planning

3. Finish this sentence:

   If I knew I could not fail, something I would like to try in the immediate future is

ON THE EDGE OF AN ADVENTURE

Then Jesus made the disciples get into the boat and go on ahead to the other side of the lake, while he sent the people away. After sending the people away, he went up a hill by himself to pray. When evening came, Jesus was there alone; and by this time the boat was far out on the lake, tossed about by the waves, because the wind was blowing against it.

Between three and six o'clock in the morning, Jesus came to the disciples, walking on the water. When they saw him walking on the water they were terrified. "It's a ghost!" they said, and screamed with fear.

Jesus spoke to them at once: "Courage!" he said. "It is I. Don't be afraid."

Then Peter spoke up. "Lord, if it is really you, order me to come out on the water to you."

"Come!" answered Jesus. So Peter got out of the boat and started walking on the water to Jesus. But when he noticed the strong wind, he was afraid and started to sink down in the water. "Save me, Lord!" he cried.

At once Jesus reached out and grabbed hold of him and said, "What little faith you have! Why did you doubt?"

They both got into the boat, and the wind died down. Then the disciples in the boat worshipped Jesus. "Truly you are the Son of God!" they exclaimed (Mt 14:22-33).

1. If I had been Peter when Jesus invited him to step out of the boat and come, I probably would have:

a. shrunk back in terror

b. asked someone else to go first

c. jumped at the chance

d. made some excuse

e. explained that I was just kidding about wanting to come

f.

2. The part of the story where I find myself right now is:

a. Needing time and space—wanting to get away from the crowd as Jesus did.

b. Trusting in God's presence—hearing the words of Jesus, "Take heart! It is I. Do not be afraid."

c. Doubting—like the disciples who can't believe it is really Jesus walking on the water.

d. Looking for a sign—asking as Peter did, "Lord, if it is you, tell me to come to you over the water."

e. Hearing a call—hearing the voice of Jesus inviting me to step out in faith and come to him.

f. Drowning—crying for help like Peter in the midst of trouble, "Save me, Lord!"

g. Believing profoundly—knowing, as did the disciples who saw the water calmed, that Jesus is God and saying, as they did, "Truly you are the Son of God!"

22

Adventures in FAiTh

This retreat is like stepping out of the boat and trusting that Jesus will help you to walk across the waters of your busy life and get closer to him.

1. How open to the retreat are you?
   I'm sitting tight in the boat. They made
   me come but I don't plan on getting wet.

I'm out splashing in the water. I want to get as much as I can out of the retreat.

2. How does the idea that Jesus invites you to "come" and get closer to him sound to you? (Circle all that apply.)

   risky   challenging
   crazy   too far out
   exciting   impossible
   corny   uninteresting
   OK but difficult   inviting

3. Evaluate your parish youth program. Tell how you felt when you first joined (circle) and how you feel about it now (box).

   a. ridiculous   h. too shallow
   b. frightening   i. demanding
   c. valuable   j. childish
   d. just what I need   k. too intellectual
   e. a waste of time   l. too "churchy"
   f. wonderful   m. good balance
   g. inadequate   n.

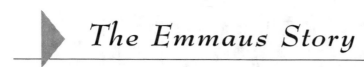

The Emmaus Story

This presentation can be used with a large group of teenagers, even as large as a school assembly or youth rally.

Materials Needed:

▸ bible

▸ copies of the "Scenarios" handout (page 28)

Directions:

1. Present a solemn reading or a dramatic presentation of the Emmaus story (Luke 24:13-35). A simple yet profound way of presenting the story is to have two people in white-face mime the parts of the two disciples as the story is read aloud. Jesus is represented only by their movements and facial expressions.

2. Give everyone a copy of the "Scenarios" handout. Say:

> The person sitting right next to you will be your partner for this activity. I'm going to tell you several stories. Each one fits a list of characters on your paper. As you're listening to each scenario, decide which character you most identify with or most sympathize with. Circle that person's name. After each story I will give you a few minutes to discuss the problem in the story with your partner.
>
> *Prom Date* Tammy is the only one of her group who hasn't been asked to prom. She's been waiting all week for Matt to call, ever since Sunday when Matt's two best friends asked her two best friends, Amy and Lisa. The phone rings, and Tammy dashes to get it. But it's not Matt; it's Kurt. Kurt works with Tammy. He's shy and studious and not very popular, but she likes talking to him. Amy and Lisa think he's a nerd. Kurt hems and haws nervously, and finally asks Tammy to go to the prom with him. *(Remind the participants to circle the name of the character they most identify with and then discuss the story with their partner.)*
>
> *Diamond Earrings* There is an uproar at the Berg family breakfast table. Mr. Berg is on the phone with the Colemans, the family where his daughter Kelly babysat last night. An expensive pair of diamond earrings is missing from Mrs. Coleman's dresser. Mr. Berg is furious. He's just shouting something about "no daughter of his is going to be accused of stealing anything" when Mrs. Berg comes out of Kelly's room with the earrings in her hand. Kelly bursts into tears. Her twin brother Mark starts making lame excuses for his sister. *(Pause for marking papers and discussion.)*
>
> *Home Sweet Home* Bob is apprehensive all the way home from school. At lunch he was telling his friends about this used motorcycle he bought in order to repair, and before he knew it he had invited everyone to come over to his

house after school to see the motorcycle and sit around the house and watch television. He knows his best buddy Joe will understand about his mom, but he's not sure what the other guys will think. After they look at the motorcycle, Bob opens the door to his house cautiously and, sure enough, the house is a mess and an empty glass that reeks of rum is right in the middle of the coffee table. His mother staggers up from the couch and says, "Hiya, honey, didja bring some friends home?" (*Pause for marking papers and discussion.*)

Party Patti Three friends are huddled together in the bathroom over Patti's half-slouched form, trying to get her to her feet. Val is really worried. This is the fourth time this month Patti has been so drunk she couldn't stand up. Val thinks they should go for some adults. Tracy is mad at Patti. It isn't even fun to go to parties with her anymore. But she is sure getting an adult in on things will just cause more problems for Patti. Kristin takes another drink of beer and giggles. She's a little buzzed herself, and thinks it's all very funny. (*Pause for marking papers and discussion.*)

Report Card Day Mr. McMullen sits at the table opening the report cards that just came in the mail. Tim has his usual straight-As with an additional note commending him for being accepted into the honor society. Dennis has gone down in everything except art. Geometry has slipped from a B+ to a D-, and he has an F in biology. Michelle, who puts in hours at her homework every night, has her usual Cs and Ds. Mr. McMullen studies the cards thoughtfully. It's so easy for Tim; Michelle tries so hard; And Dennis has so much fun! He asks himself, "What is the fairest way for me to deal with these children of mine?" (*Pause for marking papers and discussion.*)

All in the Family There are three teenagers in the Swanson family. Gretchen has a terrible temper. Ask her to do the simplest thing and if she's in a bad mood, she flies into a rage. Larry is just a grump. He'll usually help if you ask him, but he'll mope all through the job. Tom is easy-going and cheerful and really doesn't mind putzing around in the kitchen. Who will Mrs. Swanson ask to help her with the dinner dishes tonight, and tomorrow night, and the night after that? (*Pause for marking papers and discussion.*)

Football Season Coach Connelly has been at West for years. He's respected throughout the conference as a no-nonsense coach who holds to the rules, expects a lot from his teams, and yet really cares about each young man who plays for him. Good as his teams are, though, he's never won the conference title. But this is his year. Mike is the best quarterback he's ever worked with, Dave is a superb running back, and the rest of the team is strong. School spirit is mounting with each win, and the whole town is excited about the prospect of taking the conference. In a small city like Westfield the success or failure of the high school football team seems to affect everyone in town. The Monday before the season's biggest game Coach Connelly gets a phone call from the principal. Mike, Dave, and most of the senior players were busted at a beer party over the weekend. (*Pause for marking papers and discussion.*)

Caught Jodi is a good student and a sensitive caring person. Kim is a hard-working slow thinker who needs all the help she can get just to squeeze out a low C average. Jodi spends a lot of time helping her friend Kim with her homework. But last night she just didn't feel like reviewing for the history test with her. Now Jodi sits at her desk in first hour history laboring over what has turned out to be one of Mr. Kreb's heavier exams and worrying about Kim who will be taking the test third hour. There are lots of answers Kim isn't going to know and Jodi feels she is somehow responsible. She writes out a quick crib sheet to slip to her friend at class break. During the third hour exam Mr. Kreb catches Kim with the answers and recognizes Jodi's writing. His policy is to give an automatic F in the course to anyone caught cheating on his exams. *(Pause for marking papers and discussion.)*

3. After discussion time for the last scenario, ask everyone to stand and stretch. Announce a five-minute break. After the break, present a talk based on the following:

We began this session with the story of the two disciples who walked with Jesus all the way to Emmaus and didn't recognize him. Don't you wonder how that could have happened? How could they have spent several hours with their friend and not known who he was? The Emmaus story is the gospel's way of teaching us that life after the resurrection is different from life before death. Jesus was alive that Easter day, but he was alive with a new kind of life. The disciples, like all of us who have come after them, had to learn new ways to recognize him.

Imagine, if you can, being a disciple that week Jesus died. Here is this wonderful person you've known for the past three years. You've walked with him from one end of Palestine to the other. You've eaten with him around a campfire and in people's homes. You've fished with him. You've seen him cure a blind man and bring a little girl back to life. You've been amazed and puzzled and frightened and challenged by this extraordinary man. But mostly you've come to love him more than any person you've ever met.

And suddenly he's dead. Not just dead, but disgraced. He has been arrested by the authorities and executed as a criminal. You stumble through the minutes and hours, numbed with the grief of it all. Then you hear a rumor that his tomb is empty! The women say they have seen him, talked to him! You can't believe any of it. You saw the corpse yourself; he was certainly dead. You won't believe unless you see him for yourself, unless you actually touch his living body with your own two hands.

Now let's look at the same problem from Jesus' perspective. He has to convince his friends that he is a alive, that it is not just a ghost they are seeing and talking to. But he is alive in a new way. How can he convince them that from now on he will have a different kind of presence in their world, a presence that will no longer depend on the body they have been used to seeing around Galilee? He has to teach them to see in a whole new way. "I will be with you always," he tells them. "Watch for me in every stranger you meet on the road, in every hurting child, every drunken housewife, every lonely teen. You've got to learn to recognize me in all these ways or you won't know that I am alive and still with you."

There's a story I want to read to you which might make the point more clearly. It is called "The Little Fish," and it comes from a book of fables that was originally published in India (*originally published by Gujarat Sahitya Prakash, Anand, India*):

"Excuse me," said one ocean fish to another. "You are older and more experienced that I, and will probably be able to help me. Tell me: where can I find this thing they call the Ocean? I've been searching for it everywhere to no avail."

"The Ocean," said the older fish, "is what you are swimming in now."

"Oh this? But this is only water. What I am searching for is the Ocean," said the young fish, feeling quite disappointed as he swam away to search elsewhere.

Like the little fish, we need to learn to recognize a presence that fills our entire world, the presence of the risen Jesus. We have to learn that Easter is not just an event that happened once many years ago and is now over. Easter is always today. The risen Jesus is present in our world today, just waiting to be recognized and loved.

4. Have the students take out their handouts again and review the scenarios. Say:

Can you find Jesus in each story? Mark a little cross next to each character who might be suffering. That character could be the hurting Jesus. Mark a little heart next to any character who could be helpful in the situation. That character could be the helping Jesus.

5. Invite a panel of three or four students to the front of the room. They will need their handout sheets. Tell the panel:

I am going to be dialoguing with you about the scenarios on your paper. Look at them now and pick one or two that you have strong feelings about and would be willing to discuss with me. (*Pause.*) Who wants to be first?

6. Ask each panelist questions like the following:

Which scene do you want to talk about?

Who did you most identify with in that scene?

Can you recognize the helping or hurting Jesus there? Where?

What do you think should be done in cases like the one in the story?

What would you probably do in such a situation?

7. Conclude by inviting comments on that scenario from the other panelists. Then pick another panelist and repeat the questions with a second scenario. Continue until all the scenarios have been covered.

SCENARIOS

In each of the following scenarios:

▸ circle the character you most identify with or sympathize with;

▸ tell what you think that character should do.

PROM DATE
Tammy
Amy and Lisa
Matt
Kurt

HOME SWEET HOME
Bob
Joe
Friends
Mom

REPORT CARD DAY
Mr. McMullen
Tim
Michelle
Dennis

FOOTBALL SEASON
Coach Connelly
Mike
Dave
the principal
the student body

DIAMOND EARRINGS
Mrs. Berg
Mr. Berg
Kelly
Mark
Mrs. Coleman

PARTY PATTI
Patti
Val
Tracy
Kristin

ALL IN THE FAMILY
Gretchen
Larry
Tom
Mrs. Swanson

CAUGHT
Jodi
Kim
Mr. Kreb

Promises and Commitments

This presentation can be used very effectively with older teens to help them realize the importance of promises and commitments in building a successful and rewarding future.

Materials Needed:

▶ copies of the "Promises" handout (page 32)

▶ newsprint

▶ felt tip markers

▶ small pieces of paper

▶ a hat or container

Directions:

1. Give a short talk based on the following script. Prepare the talk well so you can give it in your own words using your own examples.

Script

So much in life depends on making and keeping promises. Promises are at the root of our relationships; they are often the basis of our trust in other people. Some promises are spoken—like marriage vows or an oath of office. Some are written—like a work contract or an insurance policy. Some promises are implied—the unspoken promise of constant love and care parents make to their newborn baby, or the unspoken promise to be there for practice that automatically goes with signing up for a team. We expect people to live up to the promises they make. We respect people who keep their promises, and we are rightfully disappointed and even angry with people whose word can't be depended on.

Let's take a moment now to reflect on some of the promises that touch our lives. Think of the promises, spoken and implied, that have been made to you, and the promises you have made to others. Ask God to deepen all the relationships in your life that are based on spoken and unspoken promises (*read the following list slowly allowing a bit of reflection time after each item*): the relationship with your mom . . . your dad . . . each brother and sister . . . each of your friends . . . that special boyfriend or girlfriend . . . your teammates . . . your school community . . . your parish community . . . your teachers . . . your city . . . your country . . . and most of all, your relationship with God.

2. Divide the participants into small groups. Then, say:

Let's show the people in our dialogue circles how often we make certain promises. Raise your hand to answer the following questions. How high you raise your hand tells how often you make that kind of promise. *(Read aloud the questions in Section A of the "Promises" handout, page 32, allowing time for the hand-raising after each.)*

3. Pass out pencils and copies of the "Promises" handout and say:

Now let's see what kind of promise *keepers* we are. Go back over the questions you just answered—they are in Section A of the handout—and decide how well you usually *keep* each of the promises listed. Use a 1 to 5 scale (with 1 being low and 5 being high). When you have finished, study the picture of your ratings present. Based on that picture, check one of the phrases in Section B. *(Allow time.)*

4. Next, say:

Now pick one of the promises you'd be willing to talk about to your dialogue circle. Take turns around the circle with each person talking about one kind of promise—how often you make it, how well you keep it, how you feel about yourself as a promise keeper, and so on. If you finish, go around a second and third time as you have time. The first speaker will be the one wearing the most blue. *(Allow time.)*

5. Give each circle a large sheet of poster paper or newsprint and a felt-tip marker and say:

Think for a moment of how important promises are to civilization. As a group, make a list of all of the aspects of life that require people to be true to their word. With each item you list, explain what role promises and commitments play. *(Allow time. Then post the completed lists and compare them.)*

6. Continue, say:

A commitment is a deep inner promise made either to yourself or to someone else. In the light of the importance of promises and commitments to our becoming real persons, let's do some thinking about the promises that shape our lives. Ask yourself these questions: Who or what really matters to me? Who or what am I willing to spend my time, my care, my energy, my money on? What am I committed to—what persons, groups, goals, ideals, or causes?

Move back from your circle a bit and spend some quiet time thinking about your personal commitments. As you think, fill in Section C on the "Promises" handout with names, initials, or key words. *(Allow time.)*

7. Give out small pieces of paper and ask everyone to write his or her first and last name. Collect the names in a "hat." Announce a break, and ask the group to gather after the break in a large group with their handout sheets and pencils. Gather again in a large group. Remind the participants to bring their handouts and pencils. Take up the "hat" full of names and say:

I will draw a name from this hat. The person whose name is picked is "on the spot." I will ask that person some questions about the commitments he or she was thinking about earlier. We do have a pass rule. If you are asked a question you don't want to answer, you simply say "Pass." If you choose to respond, however, your answer should be as honest as possible.

8. Draw a name and ask two or three questions. Then draw another name, and so forth. Some sample questions are listed below.

Questions

▸ Would you tell us about a relationship you are committed to? (*You might substitute "team" or "idea" for "relationship."*)

▸ How long have you been involved in this commitment?

▸ How does this commitment affect your life?

▸ How firm is the commitment?

▸ How much time, energy, and money do you spend on it?

▸ What kinds of things might weaken the commitment?

▸ Is it possible that it might die out completely?

▸ How public is your commitment?

▸ How much does your commitment affect other people?

Promises

A. How often do you

▼ promise your mom you'll clean your room?
▼ promise to do better on your next report card? _____
▼ promise to take a little brother or sister somewhere? _____
▼ promise to get home early with the car? _____
▼ promise to write to someone going away? _____
▼ promise you won't tell a secret? _____
▼ promise to pay back money you've borrowed? _____
▼ promise to do the dishes—"later"? _____
▼ promise God you'll do something for him? _____
▼ promise to stay out of trouble? _____
▼ promise yourself you'll make a change? _____
▼ promise someone you'll "go steady"? _____

Using a 1 to 5 scale, rate yourself as a promise keeper in each case above.

B. When you say the words "I promise," what do they mean?

_____ I have given my word and I will follow through no matter what.

_____ I'll try to do the thing I said I would.

_____ I might do what I said if it's not too inconvenient.

_____ I say the words lightly; they don't mean anything.

_____ Other: _____

C. A commitment is a deep inner promise made either to yourself or to others. List some of your personal commitments in the boxes below.

person or relationship	team or organization	job or task
goal	ideal or value	cause

32

Value Systems

This presentation and related activities always engenders an excellent large-group discussion. It helps the participants look closely at some of their personal values—to see where they came from, how they are influenced by family and friends, and what it costs to live according to them.

Materials and Preparation Needed:

▸ lap pads

▸ copies of "Friendship Frame" and "Value Indicators" handouts (pages 36 and 37)

Directions:

1. Begin the session in a large, informal group, sitting on the floor, if possible. (The whole session can be conducted in the large group, or you can break into small groups for discussion later in the session.)

2. Pass out copies of the "Friendship Frame" handout (page 36) and say:

   Look at the exercise labeled "Friendship Frame." In a minute I'll ask you to put the initials of your friends in the frame. Where you put the initials shows where that friend fits in your friendship group. Closest to the word *me*, put the initials of the people who usually hang around with you. You may add initials for other clusters of friends—from work, from the band, from the crew of the school play, from summer camp.

   Fill in your friendship frame now. (*Allow a few minutes for filling in the friendship frame.*)

3. Pass out copies of "Value Indicators" (page 37) and say:

   Now look at these values indicators. This list of activities indicates the values held by an individual or a group (though some of the items on the list would be more accurately defined as vices). How is each item viewed by the people whose names you just put in the friendship frame? Use the number code at the right to show whether the item is "in" or "out" in your group. Mark your answers in the first column. You may want to consult with your friends as you work down the list. (*Allow time.*)

4. When everyone has finished marking the list, say:

   Now let's share some of our ratings. I'll call an item and you show by raising your fingers how you think your friends would rate that item. Where does your group stand on No. 1, obeying rules? (*Pause.*) On No. 11, driving drunk or stoned? (*Pause.*) On No. 23, "BS" ing teachers? (*Pause.*) Are there any other items you would like to see the group's rating on? (*Call for the ratings on a few items suggested by the group. Do not discuss the issues at this time.*)

5. Say:

Now we are going to go through the list a second time rating each item according to the value system you were *taught*—by your parents, your religion teachers, your school. Put the rating in the second column. If you weren't taught anything about a particular item, just leave that line blank. (*Allow time.*)

6. After the group is finished, say:

Now compare the two lists. In how many items is there a difference between the values you have been taught and the values your friends hold? When you have your total, just say it aloud. (*Pause for responses.*)

7. When all have finished counting, say:

Raise your hand if you had a difference in more than 35 items . . . 30 to 35 . . . 25 to 30 . . . less than 25.

8. Continue with a deeper presentation on how we learn values. Say:

Let's look more deeply at the question, How do we learn values? Our values come from various sources. Some values are *taught*. Your parents, your religious leaders, and your teacher have been trying to get you to learn and live by a definite set of values since you were very little. You know those values very well—no one had any trouble filling in the second column on the chart—but if you're like the rest of us you probably don't live by them all the time.

Other values are *caught* from the people we spend our time with, especially our families and our friends. Catching values is a natural phenomenon. It isn't bad or good, it just is. Because we are social beings, we adapt to the ideas, attitudes, actions, and values of the people around us. We catch both positive and negative values from others. If the people around us are kind and friendly, we tend to be kind and friendly. If everyone is crabby or negative, we can easily be the same. If cheating on tests, picking on unpopular kids, and cutting down teachers are acceptable actions in our friendship group, it's easy for us to do those things. On the other hand, we can also get caught up in such positive actions as planning a surprise party for a teacher, working on a benefit walk, or gathering food for the poor.

When this phenomenon of catching values is mostly negative, it's called peer pressure. When it's positive, we are likely to call it good example. In either case, it is a natural part of life for everyone, adults as well as teenagers. But that doesn't mean we don't have any control over the values we catch from our peers. We need to look critically at the values of the people around us and to make definite choices about which values we want to accept and imitate and which we want to reject.

That brings us to a third source of values, those we choose for ourselves. We will call those our *thought* values. We can't go through life just doing unthinkingly whatever we have been *taught*. Nor should we act unthinkingly on the values we have *caught* from our peers. We need to *think* about the values in both of those categories, to weigh them against our own experience and understanding, and to choose for ourselves the values which will direct our lives. If we don't make thought-filled choices about life, someone else, either our families or our friends, will be doing our thinking for us.

9. Say:

Now let's fill in the last column on the "Value Indicators" chart. Go through the list again and think: Where do I stand on this item? Where does this item rate in my personal value system?

Do this exercise quietly. When you and a friend have both finished the list, share your answers and discuss any differences.

Friendship Frame

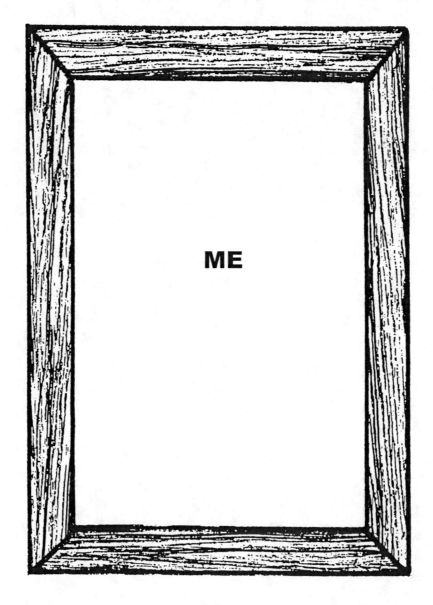

ME

Value Indicators

1. Obeying rules
2. Joining a club
3. Going to class drunk or high
4. Reading the bible
5. Wearing expensive, fashionable clothes
6. Helping teachers
7. Sex before marriage
8. Telling crude jokes
9. Shoplifting
10. Cutting down teachers
11. Driving drunk or stoned
12. Gossiping about peers
13. Talking about God
14. Helping the poor
15. Cheating on schoolwork
16. Bad-mouthing religion
17. Bragging about sexual conquests
18. Going out for sports
19. Getting good grades
20. Smoking cigarettes

21. Chastity and abstinence
22. Lying to parents
23. "BS"ing teachers
24. Dressing up for school
25. Going to church
26. Abortion
27. Unchaperoned parties
28. Putting down unpopular kids
29. Being lazy and uncaring
30. Fighting
31. Using good table manners
32. Smoking pot
33. Singing in church
34. Looking at pornography
35. Driving above the speed limit
36. Being polite to adults
37. Eating healthy foods
38. Assisting a neighbor in need
39. Visiting with a grandparent
40. Going willingly on a family vacation

IN

5 — Praised!

4 — Encouraged

3 — Accepted

2 — Tolerated

1 — Rejected

OUT

Parable of the Sower

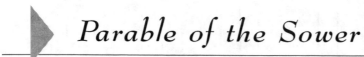

This presentation with exercises works well at the end of a retreat. Its purpose is to help the participants think about how they will carry the effects of the retreat into their everyday lives.

Materials and Preparations Needed:

▸ a cast of eleven volunteers for the dramatic presentation (allow about five minutes for practice). Cast in order of appearance:

Narrator/Farmer (someone who reads well)

Seed Sown Along the Path (a small person)

Bird (someone strong enough to carry Seed Sown Along the Path)

Seed Sown in Rocky Ground

Sun

Thorn Seed One

Thorn Seed Two

Seed Sown Among Thorns (should be the opposite sex from Thorn Seed Two)

Seed Which Falls in Good Soil One

Seed Which Falls in Good Soil Two

Seed Which Falls in Good Soil Three

▸ props: a blanket, three beanbag chairs or floor cushions, and one chair

▸ a copy of the "Parable of the Sower Script" (pages 41-42) for the narrator.

▸ a copy of the "Parable of the Sower" handout (page 43) for each participant

▸ a copy of the "Seed Prayer" handout (page 44) for each participant

▸ a package of small seeds (mustard seeds if possible)

Directions:

1. Gather the audience. The narrator/farmer begins reading the script from "Parable of the Sower Script." The other cast members come on stage as their parts appear.

2. After the reading, give out the "Parable of Sower" handouts and pencils, and say:

Our time together is a special seed-planting time. We have witnessed how God's word has been planted in your hearts in many ways. For some of you, this may have been the richest planting time of your lives. But seeds need to be cared for if they are to grow. A retreat can make a real difference in a person's life, or it can be an experience that is forgotten the minute the person walks out the door. This exercise is meant to help you think about the obstacles to faith that will be waiting for you when you get back home. It will suggest some ways you can overcome these obstacles.

First, I'd like you to think about the *sowers* in your lives. Over the years, what people and events have planted the seeds of Christian faith in your heart? Write these in the first space on your handout. Most of you can write the names of family members—parents, grandparents, perhaps an older brother or sister. And maybe there is a special teacher or priest or some other admired adult who has encouraged you to live a truly Christian life. Some of you may have peers who inspire you and give you a good example. Or maybe your inspiration has come from books or movies. For some, it may have been a death or tragedy that opened your heart to *hear* God's word.

3. Allow sufficient time to reflect on and write the names of the "sowers," then say:

Now talk to your table group about some of your seed planters. Take turns around the circle. Each person talk about one "sower" each round. Tell how that person reached your heart with God's word.

4. When all have talked about at least one of their responses, say:

Now let's think about some of those *obstacles* that keep us from living the kind of Christian lives we know we should live. Why doesn't God's word get through to us more often or more deeply? The parable gives us three kinds of reasons: First, there are the "birds," the people who swoop into our lives and snatch God's word away. Sometimes the birds are friends with negative attitudes; they laugh at us if we start taking religion too seriously. Sometimes the negativity is more subtle: you just have a feeling that faith isn't too acceptable in your peer group. Sometimes the birds who make faith difficult are within our own families, even our parents might subtly discourage us from taking God too seriously. Other "birds" might be things that make us *doubt* God's word: people we know who are skeptical about religion; books, movies, even classes in school that make us wonder about our faith.

Who or what are some "birds" in your life? Write your responses beside the illustration of a bird on the handout.

5. Allow time to write ideas in the "bird" box, but don't discuss them at this time. Then, say:

The birds represent things *outside* ourselves that take God's word out of our hearts and minds, but there is a *second* set of reasons we don't grow in faith. These reasons are *within* us. Our own souls are sometimes so rocky that God can't get through to us. Let's think of some of the circumstances that might be counted as rocky soil: Perhaps we have a bad attitude toward religion. Maybe we are just lazy or bored. It could be simple inattention; God's word may not touch our hearts because we never *listen* to it. Maybe some bad experience in the past—a painful death, a divorce, a broken relationship, serious sin—has caused us to harden our hearts against God.

What are some things that could be "rocky ground" for you? Write your response in the "rocks" on the handout.

6. Allow time, but don't share yet. Continue:

Third, the parable talks about thorns, the things in our life, good or bad, that seem to crowd God out. Life has a way of keeping us so busy or involved that we just don't have time for God. In this space we can list things like school, work, relationships, sports, popularity, music, TV, parties, worries—anything that takes up the time we should be giving to God, anything that begins to take precedence in our lives over God and our relationship with him.

7. Again, allow time for marking. Then, say:

Look over the last three boxes now—"birds," "rocky soil," and "thorns"—and pick out one obstacle that you think might keep this retreat time from making a real difference in your life. Share that with your group.

8. After the sharing, continue. Say:

And now, let's think about some of the ways we can overcome those obstacles, some of the things we can do to care for the seeds that were planted during our time together. What are some definite changes you want to make in your life? You might promise God and yourself more prayer time, or better Mass attendance. Maybe there is someone you need to forgive, someone you want to talk to, someone you could be kinder to. Maybe a certain attitude needs to be improved, or a habit has to be changed—gutter language, alcohol consumption, study habits.

In the last space, list five things you hope to change.

9. After allowing time, conclude this portion of the presentation. Say:

Now look back over the last box and pick one of the five changes that you are really committed to doing something about. Sharing that one with your group will strengthen your resolve. Try to be very specific in telling what you want to do to keep your retreat promises alive.

10. Next, have the participants gather at small-group discussion tables. Pass out copies of the "Seed Prayer" and have them put the prayer on the table in front of them. Then walk among the group, silently "planting" a seed in each person's hand. (Place the seed on the palm, and then gently close the person's finger over it. Smile a blessing upon each person before moving to the next.) When everyone has a seed, say:

Please put your seeds together in the center of the table. Then put your right hands in a pile on top of them. (*Allow time.*) The seeds of this retreat are now planted under your hands. The love and faith you share as a group will provide the heat they need to grow. Let's ask God to keep the spirit of our time together alive for all of us by praying together the prayer on the handout sheet:

"Lord Jesus, you have planted your word in our hearts. It is a word of love and of challenge, a word that will bring us both support and struggle. We have listened to your word. We trust in your faithful care for us. Please help us to allow the seeds of your love to grow more deeply and firmly in our lives. Amen."

Parable of the Sower Script

Narrator/Farmer:

The (*name of your group*) Gospel Players present: "The Parable of the Sower."

At that time Jesus began to teach beside Lake Galilee. The crowd that gathered around him (*narrator points to the audience*) was so large that he got into a boat (*narrator "rows away" a few paces*) and spoke to the crowd on the shore at the water's edge. This is what he said:

Listen! Once there was a man who went out to sow grain (*narrator scatters seeds around*). As he scattered the seed in the field, some of it fell along the path (*Seed Sown Along the Path enters and crouches in a "planted" position*), and the birds came and ate it up. (*Bird swoops in wearing a blanket as wings and carries off Seed Sown Along the Path.*)

Some of the seed fell on rocky ground where there was little soil. (*Seed Sown on Rocky Ground enters and crouches; the rest of the cast throws beanbag chairs or pillows around Seed.*) The seed soon sprouted because the soil wasn't deep. Then, when the sun came up (*Sun enters, stands on chair and beams hot rays down on Seed Sown on Rocky Ground*), it burned the young plants, and because the roots had not grown deep enough, the plants soon dried up (*Seed Sown on Rocky Ground collapses*).

Some seed fell among thorn bushes, (*Thorns One and Two enter and get "planted"; Seed Sown Among the Thorns crouches between them*) which grew up (*Seeds grow*) and choked the plant (*Thorns One and Two choke Seed; Seed collapses*), and they didn't bear grain.

But some seed fell in good soil (*enter the three Seeds Which Fall in Good Soil*), and the plants sprouted, grew and bore grain: some had thirty grains (*Good Seed One happily flashes 30 with his or her fingers*), others sixty (*Good Seed Two flashes 60*), and the others one hundred (*Good Seed Three flashes 100*).

And Jesus said: "Listen, then, if you have ears!" (*All cast members move off to get ready for the second half of the parable.*) However, the people (*narrator points to the audience*) did not understand, and so Jesus explained the parable to them:

The sower sows God's message. Some people are like the seeds that fall along the path (*Seed Sown Along the Path enters*); as soon as they hear the message, Satan comes (*Birds swoop in*) and takes it away.

Other people are like the seeds that fall on rocky ground (*enter Seed Sown in Rocky Ground; toss in beanbags or pillows*). As soon as they hear the message, they receive it gladly. But it does not sink deep into them, and they don't last long. So when trouble or persecution comes (*enter Sun*) because of the message, they give it up at once.

Other people are like the seeds sown among the thorn bushes (*enter Thorns and Seed*). These are the ones who hear the message, but the worries about this life, the love for riches (*Thorn One tempts Seed with some money*), and all other kinds of desires (*Thorn Two makes a sexual advance*) crowd in and choke the message.

But other people are like the seeds sown in good soil (*Good Seeds enter*). They hear the message, accept it and bear fruit: some thirty, some sixty, and some one hundred!" (*Good seeds repeat actions, flashing 30, 60, and 100 with their fingers.*)

The Word of the Lord.

PARABLE OF THE Sower

"Once there was a man who went out to sow grain . . . "

Name the "sowers" in your life—the persons who have planted the Word of God in your soil.

"Some seed fell along the path, and the birds came and ate it up . . . "

In your life, who or what are the "birds" that snatch the seed of God away before it gets a chance to sprout?

"Some seed fell on rocky ground where there was little soil . . . "

What might cause a person to be rocky soil, one who hears the word, begins to practice it, but soon gives up?

"Some of the seed fell among thorn bushes which grew up and choked the plant . . . "

What are the "thorns" in your life—the worries or desires or activities that seem to crowd Christ out?

"But some seeds fell in good soil, and the plants sprouted, grew, and bore grain . . . "

What definite things could you do *each day* to keep the seeds of Christianity growing and yielding fruit in your life?

List five.
* Put at star next to the one you have definitely decided you *will* do.

43

Seed Prayer

Lord Jesus, You have planted your word in our hearts. It is a word of love and of challenge, a word that will bring us both support and struggle. We have listened to your word. We trust in your faithful care for us. Please help us to allow the seeds of your love to grow more deeply and firmly in our lives.

AMEN.

COMMUNITY

BUILDING

Stand If . . .

Directions:

▸ While the participants are seated, say:

Before I begin today, I need to know about this group. I'll ask you some questions; you answer by standing at the appropriate time.

Stand if you're a senior.

    Remain standing if you think you might still be a senior next year.

Stand if you're a sophomore.

    Remain standing if you think freshmen are cute.

Stand if you're a freshman.

    Remain standing if you think seniors are wonderful.

Stand if you think the juniors are the best class in the school.

    Remain standing if you think the rest of the school agrees with you.

Stand if you think teachers give too much homework.

    Remain standing if you do it all anyway.

Stand if you've ever been on a blind date.

    Remain standing if it developed into a real relationship.

Stand if you've ever been skinny dipping.

    Remain standing if it was daylight.

Stand if you have a paying job.

    Remain standing if you put money in the bank each week.

Stand if you've been grounded in the last month.

    Remain standing if you deserved it.

Stand if you willingly apologize when you're wrong.

    Stand if you're never wrong.

Stand if you have a little brother or sister who acts like a brat sometimes.

    Remain standing if you love the little stinker anyway.

Stand if the friendship groups in your school are "cliquey."

    Remain standing if your group is a clique.

Stand if you have ever felt left out and alone.

    Remain standing if you go out of your way to welcome outsiders into your group.

Stand if you think you've had enough exercise during this activity.

    Remain standing if you already ran ten miles today.

If, If, If

Directions:

▶ Use these series of statements as an ice-breaker or as a fun exercise during break time. Say:

If you have your own savings account, raise your right hand.

If there's anything in it, raise both hands.

If you'd like to try hang-gliding, flap your wings.

If you talk on the phone at least five hours a week, hold your right ear in your hand.

If you're a friendly, outgoing person, shake hands with three people near you.

If you're shy, cover your face with your hands (keep it covered for the next "if").

If you're not at all shy, kiss someone whose face is covered.

If you can lift 50 pounds, flex your muscles.

If you can lift 150 pounds, pick up the person next to you.

If you told a lie this week, slap your mouth.

If you've got smelly feet, hold your nose.

If in the past week you said the words "I'm sorry" and meant them, raise your left hand.

If you said the words "I love you," cross your heart with your hands.

If you said the words "It was my fault," point a thumb at your chest.

If you usually pray before you go to bed, fold your hands.

If you play a musical instrument, pretend you're playing it.

If you're the baby of the family, suck your thumb.

If you think we've had enough of these personal revelations, stand up.

Team Juggling

Materials and Preparations Needed:

▶ a small beanbag, hackiesac, or folded, clean pair of socks for each participant

Directions

1. Have each small group stand in a circle around its table. Put the beanbags for the group in one pile on the table.

2. The play goes like this: Bill picks up one beanbag and tosses it across the circle to Mary, saying Mary's name as he does so. Mary tosses the bag across the circle to Fred, calling out Fred's name. Fred tosses it to Joan, and so on, until everyone in the group has received the beanbag. The last person to get the bag tosses it back to Bill, again saying Bill's name, and the bag—and the names—continue being tossed around in the same pattern. When the pattern is flowing smoothly, Bill picks up a second bag, tosses it to Mary, again saying her name, and starts the second bag moving in the same pattern. When the second bag is moving smoothly, Bill starts a third, and so on, until all the bags are in motion.

3. If someone breaks the pattern by dropping a beanbag, the group starts again with one bag, and begins again to gradually build up the number of bags they are juggling. The aim of the game is to see how many bags each group can set in motion.

Trust Walk

Preparation and Materials Needed:

- ▶ a blindfold for each participant (except the group leaders)
- ▶ several copies of the "Trust Walk Directions" (page 51) for the guides
- ▶ group leaders, one for every six or seven participants
- ▶ several playground balls
- ▶ several jump ropes
- ▶ copies of the "Trust" handout (page 52)

Directions:

1. Gather the group, preferably outdoors, and say:

   Help each other put on these blindfolds. Fasten them securely because the exercise won't be effective if you can see even a little. When you are blindfolded, sit down and wait for further directions. *(Everyone gets a blindfold except the group leaders.)*

2. Continue your explanation of the activity:

   I would like you to sit here silently, imagining what it must be like to be blind. In your mind go through just one day and think how that day would be if you couldn't see at all *(read the following slowly, pausing between phrases)*: waking in the morning, taking a shower, selecting your clothes, fixing your hair, putting on makeup, preparing breakfast, going to school, recognizing your friends, attending classes, participating in your favorite sports, listening to music, doing homework, going to parties, going to bed. Since you can't see, try to experience your other senses more keenly. What can you hear? How do things feel and smell and taste?

   Soon someone will come, take you by the hand, and lead you on a sensory journey. Go with your guide and do whatever he or she guides you to do. You will have to trust that your guide cares about you and will not let you get hurt. The walk will be done in *complete silence*, so you will have to rely totally on your guide and your own senses of hearing, touch, smell, and taste. Wait now, as patiently as you can, for someone to come to you. It is important that everyone keep perfect silence throughout this activity.

3. Give each leader a copy of the "Directions for Guides" (page 51). Ask the leaders to read the directions, then select one blindfolded person to lead on a sensory journey. Continue until all the "blind" have been taken on a walk.

4. After the walks, give everyone a copy of the "Trust" handout (page 52). Ask the participants to spend some quiet time thinking about the meaning of the trust walk experience and answering the questions.

5. Gather in a large group to share the reflections.

Directions for Guides:

Trust Walk

- ▸ Select a "blind" person, one of the opposite sex if possible

- ▸ Keep perfect silence

- ▸ Lead your person through many different experiences:

    touch things of various textures

    go up and down stairs

    listen to noises

    smell flowers, leaves

    bounce a ball; play simple catch; jump rope

    (add other appropriate experiences)

- ▸ Stay within sight of the retreat director

- ▸ Be gentle; be careful; be trustworthy

- ▸ Try not to give yourself away

- ▸ Bring the person back to the group and remove the blindfold

- ▸ Show the person the directions and ask him or her to take one of the remaining blindfolded people for a walk

- ▸ Select another person to take for a walk

TRUST WALK REFLECTION SHEET

Trust

1. Describe the feelings you had as you were led on the trust walk.

2. What was your most significant experience during the trust walk?

3. What did you discover about yourself during this walk?

4. Describe your partner, basing your impressions totally on what you experienced during the trust walk.

5. What kind of guide were _you_—patient, mean, irresponsible, trust-worthy, caring, gentle, teasing?

6. Did this trust walk bring to mind any experience from your past? Describe briefly.

Nametag Introductions

Materials and Preparation Needed:

▸ a few wideline markers

▸ a large nametag (about 4" x 4") for each person

▸ pins

Directions:

1. Have the participants sit where they choose at dialogue tables. (This means they will automatically sit according to friendship groups.) Later the group will move to a large-group area, and then back to the dialogue tables. Say:

    Please use a wideline marker to print your *first* name on the name tag. (*Allow time.*) Now take a pencil and write or draw the following items on the name tag, on the same side as your name. There will be ten items (*allow time to draw each*): 1) draw a picture of your favorite childhood toy, 2) draw a picture to stand for your favorite activity now, 3) write a childhood nickname, 4) write the name of your best friend and a one-word description of him or her, 5) write the name of an adult you admire, 6) draw a teardrop and write next to it the date of the last time you cried, 7) draw a hand and write next to it the date of the last year you got spanked, 8) draw a key and write next to it the date of the last time you got grounded, 9) write three words that finish this sentence: "My friends think I'm . . . ", 10) name your favorite symbol for God: for example, wind, fire, rock, light, air.

2. Say:

    Bring your name tag and move to the large-group area. On the way, pair up with someone who was *not* sitting at your table. Sit with that person in the large-group area. Find a partner of the opposite sex if possible. (*Discreetly tell the adults to hold back a minute so they can choose as partners any teenagers being left out.*)

3. When all are settled, say:

    Now give your name tag to your partner and take turns explaining the symbols and words to each other. Talk about one item at a time. Listen carefully, because you will be using what you learn about your partner to introduce him or her to the entire group.

4. After the partners have talked, say:

    Look at your partner's name tag again and select the three most interesting items to tell us all about. (*Allow time.*) Now, introduce your partner to the group saying something like: "This is Tom Jones. I just learned that. . . ."

Sentence Starters

Materials and Preparations Needed:

▸ eight of the sentence starters below written on the chalkboard or chart

Sentence Starters

Someday I hope to . . .

It upsets me when . . .

I admire people who . . .

It is important to me that . . .

I wish I could change . . .

Sometimes I wonder why . . .

I am convinced that . . .

I hope I never . . .

I am trying to improve my character by . . .

People would like me better if . . .

I am afraid that . . .

I get discouraged when . . .

When I don't get my way I . . .

I would like to tell _____ that . . .

I'm sorry about . . .

I am happiest when . . .

I complain a lot about . . .

The last time I cried was . . .

I have definitely decided to . . .

When I hurt someone, I . . .

I'm proud of _____ because . . .

When people tease me, I . . .

▸ cards ace through 8 from a deck of cards

Directions:

1. Gather in the large-group setting. Ask the participants to sit where they can see the sentence starters on the board.

2. Have everyone think up an adjective to describe himself or herself. The adjective must begin with the same letter as the person's name, e.g., "Energetic Ellen" or "Dapper Douglas." When everyone's ready, say:

    Spend a few minutes deciding what you might say if you were called on to finish each of the sentences on the board. Think of endings that tell us something important about you and your values. You can work together with a friend to think up your answers.

3. When most are ready, say:

    I have in my hand the numbers from 1 to 8. When it is almost your turn, I will pull a number to tell you which sentence you are going to finish for us. You will be told your number one turn ahead so you have a minute to get your thoughts together.

4. Pick the numbers for the first two people. Because the first answers will set the tone for the whole exercise, start with teens who are likely to give serious answers. Say to Person A, "Tell us your adjective and your name." Repeat the name and say, "Brave Bill, what is your answer to number 4?" Listen to the person's answer and ask one or two follow-up questions. Before beginning to talk to Person B, select a number for Person C.

5. Ask every fifth person or so to repeat the names and adjectives as far back as he or she can.

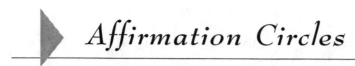

Affirmation Circles

This is a must exercise for the closing hours of a two- or three-day retreat. It gives the young people and group leaders an opportunity to receive a hearty dose of positive affirmation from their new friends.

Preparation Needed:

▶ Allow plenty of time, since the activity could last anywhere from 30 to 60 minutes.

Directions:

1. Gather in the large-group area setting for the following introductions and directions. Say:

   This retreat has been a time out in the game of life we play each day. During the retreat we've been looking at how we usually play the game and deciding on some of the ways we want to make a change. One of the "plays" all of us seem to need a lot of practice in is affirming people, telling others the things about them that are special and good. And most of us also need some practice in accepting affirmation without getting all flustered and embarrassed. The next exercise will give us practice in both giving and receiving affirmation. This is how it works:

   Gather in your small group cozy corners. Decide on one person (someone who isn't too shy, like Jim, for instance) to be the first affirmee. Then everyone sit for a moment thinking about what it is that makes Jim the special and unique person that he is—the qualities, gifts, talents, mannerisms, and personality traits that make Jim Jim. After you've had time to think, everyone tells Jim something positive about him. Try to talk right *to* the person. Say, "What I like about you, Jim is . . ." not "What's nice about Jim is. . . ." Jim just sits there, soaking it all in. Only after everyone has spoken can the affirmee respond. To respond just thank your group, and then tell them a little about the kind of person you are trying to become.

   The person who was just affirmed picks the next affirmee and gives the first affirmation. Everyone again spends a few minutes thinking quietly before beginning to affirm the new person.

   When you have affirmed everyone in your group, stay in your corners chatting quietly till all the groups are finished.

2. When you are sure the directions have been understood, have everyone move to the small-group cozy corners to begin the affirmation exercise.

3. Visit each group briefly to be sure the process is being followed correctly.

Mail Bags

This is a fine activity for helping young people learn to pay positive attention to other people and to be affirming of one another.

Materials and Preparations Needed:

▸ one paper bag (lunch bag size) for each person

▸ a set of colored marking pens for each table

▸ a large supply of 3" x 5" papers

▸ a recording of a song with lyrics that speak of friendship and love

Directions:

1. Take time to create and explain the mail bags early in the retreat. Give each person a paper bag and say:

    This bag will be your personal mail bag during the retreat. Put your name on it and decorate it. Then line the bags up on the ledge (or tape them to the wall) in alphabetical order by first names.

2. Point out where you have put the supply of note paper and say:

    All during the retreat, I would like you to pay very special attention to all the very special people who are here on retreat with you. When you notice something good about someone, write a little note telling the person about the special quality, attitude, or action that you have been noticing. Sign your name to your note and put it in the person's mailbag.

    Write a note to every person in your small group, and to as many other people as you wish. Please, do not look at the notes in your own bag; they will be presented at a special ceremony later in the retreat.

3. Check the bags occasionally. If someone is not receiving many notes, make sure you and some of the other leaders write to that person.

4. Toward the end of the retreat gather everyone in one large circle. Give out the mail bags randomly so that everyone has a bag, but no one has his or her own. Say:

    Each of us holds in our hands a bag full of love and good wishes. In a few minutes you will be delivering that bag to its owner. When it is your turn, walk over to the person whose mail bag you have, deliver the bag, and give the person a big hug from all of us. Then the person who just got hugged will deliver a bag and a hug, and the chain will keep going until everyone has received his or her mail bag and has been duly hugged.

Please, do not start reading your mail until after the ceremony.

5. When all the mail bags have been delivered, say:

Put your arms around each others shoulders and listen to (the song you have chosen with lyrics speaking of friendship and love). Sing along if you can.

Enjoy your mail!

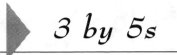

3 by 5s

Materials and Preparations Needed:

▸ one set of the 3 by 5 handouts (page 60) for each participant. Cut the 3 by 5s apart and assemble them so that each person receives a complete set of twelve papers.

Directions:

1. Distribute the sets. Say:

Everyone has a set of twelve papers, each containing a dialogue starter. Spend the next twenty minutes or so in an "alone" spot thinking about the starters and writing responses to them.

2. After the reflection time, gather in the large-group setting. Say:

Look at your twelve papers. Arrange them in order so that your better, more thought-out answers are on top. When it's your turn to share, talk to us about one of your responses; don't read it to us.

3. Call on someone to start. Dialogue with the person for a few minutes about what he or she shares, then ask the person to pick someone of the opposite sex to respond next.

3 by 5s

If I could go back to do my high school years over, I would . . .

I'm really grateful to my teachers for . . .

I owe it to the church to . . .

This year I improved my attitude about . . .

After leaving high school I will continue to live my Catholic faith by . . .

One thing about Catholic Christianity that I still don't understand is . . .

Next year I hope to . . .

I'd like to tell the senior class that . . .

At this stage in my life I can see that I need the church for . . .

People would have liked me better this year if . . .

Something about my school that disappointed me this year was . . .

One reason why I'm glad to be a Catholic Christian is . . .

DISCUSSIONS & EXERCISES

My Personal Values

Materials Needed:

▸ a small, blank card for each participant

Directions:

1. Write on the board several typical values and vices held by teens (e.g., reading the Bible, using vulgar language, exercising, cheating on tests, studying for tests). May more values and vices of teens are listed on the handout "Value Indicators" (page 37).

2. Say:

   If you really value something, you're willing to talk about the value openly and if necessary defend your position in the face of questions or opposition. Look at the values listed on the board. Make a mental note of three or four items you have a strong position on and would be willing to talk about in front of the whole group.

3. Give the participants small cards on which to write their first and last names. Collect the cards. Say:

   I will draw someone's name from this pack. If your name is picked, you will be "on the spot" and will be asked to explain your position on one of the items you chose. Decide which item you will talk about if your name is picked.

4. Pull a name and ask several questions like:

   What item do you want to talk about?

   What is your position on _____?

   Do your peers agree with that position? your parents?

   Have you felt that way for a long time or is it something you've come to only recently?

5. Conclude by asking if anyone else has a question or response for the person on the spot.

6. Continue with as many persons as time allows.

Alternate Directions:

1. Have the participants move to small dialogue groups. Say:

> Each of you will have a chance now to find out where the people in your small group stand on an issue of your choice. Take turns around the circle. When it is your turn select one item from the items listed on the board and ask each person in your group to comment on that issue. Explain your own position in response to their comments.

Show Your Hand

Directions:

1. Sit at dialogue tables. Say:

   I will read aloud some controversial statements. As each is read, tell your group how you feel about the statement by the number of fingers you show on the table:

   5 fingers mean you totally agree

   4 fingers mean you agree somewhat

   3 fingers mean you can't make up your mind

   2 fingers mean you disagree somewhat

   1 finger means you definitely disagree (Use your pinky, please!)

   a fist means pass; you don't want to express your opinion at this time

   (Review the code one more time before continuing.)

2. Continue:

   The process works like this: Everyone puts his or her right fist on the table. I will read a statement and give you a minute to think. Then we will all knock on the table three times counting: one, two, three, show. After the three count, we all show our answers. Ready to try it? Put your right fist on the table. First statement: Girls and women are more religious than men and boys. Think a minute. Knock together: One, two, three, show. Now look at everyone's answer and discuss the statement. If someone showed a 1 and someone else a 5, those two should begin by explaining their positions to one another. *(Allow a few minutes for discussion.)*

3. Continue with statements such as the ones below. Discussion time on each can be longer or shorter depending on the interest of the group.

   Women are entitled to equal rights in all areas of society.

   Marijuana should be legalized.

   I want to marry a virgin.

   I came to this retreat (class) because I wanted to.

   Drunk drivers should be charged with a felony.

   Jesus walked on water.

Priests should be allowed to marry.

If men are drafted, women should be drafted.

Sex should be saved for marriage.

This is boring.

Sunday Mass should be optional.

We each have to decide for ourselves what is right and wrong.

I pray every day.

Students who attend a Christian school are more religious than public school students.

I belong to a "huggy" family.

I like strict teachers.

Families should go to church together on Sunday.

I like winter.

I go to school because I want to.

I go to church because I want to.

Teenagers should be punished when they misbehave.

I should be punished when I misbehave.

Skateboarding is not a crime.

I think of God often.

God punishes me when I'm bad.

I expect to go to heaven when I die.

Jesus is alive right now.

People are basically good.

Jesus is my personal friend.

Lying to teachers is necessary.

Lying to parents is necessary.

My parents trust me.

My parents should trust me.

Teenagers should have a definite curfew.

Teenagers who break curfew should be grounded.

Teenagers with jobs should help pay family expenses.

I really try to make my family happy.

I would allow my freshman (sophomore, junior, senior) son to date.

I would allow my freshman (sophomore, junior, senior) daughter to date.

I willingly do my fair share of the family chores.

Our family discusses problems rationally.

4. You can vary the discussion patterns by saying things like:

    This time the oldest person in the group discuss with the youngest.

    This time only the blue-eyed people talk and the browns listen.

    This time everyone explain the meaning of your response.

Cozy Corner Questions

This is an excellent activity for getting the group to share openly and deeply. Allow at least 45 minutes for it; you could spend as long as 90 minutes. The questions work well as a late-night exercise on the opening night of a retreat.

Materials and Preparations Needed:

▸ a copy of the "Cozy Corner Directions" (page 71) for each group leader

▸ one set of "Cozy Corner Questions" (pages 72-77) for each dialogue group

Directions:

1. Assign each small group to a "cozy corner"—a comfortable spot where the participants can sit around in a circle on floor pillows or couches. Give each group leader a set of cards and a copy of the directions. Assign a closing time.

Cozy Corner Directions

1. Put the cards face down in the center of the group.

2. *Person A* picks two cards, reads them silently, chooses one and decides to whom to direct the question. *Person A* then reads the question directly to *Person B*, for example, "John, what do you believe happens to the human person after death?"

3. *Person B* answers the question. *Person A* then responds, by agreeing or disagreeing, by giving his or her own answer, by asking a follow-up question, and so forth.

4. *Person A* then asks if anyone else in the group wants to comment. *Person A* might also ask to hear *everyone's* answer to the question.

5. *Person B* selects two questions and proceeds as above.

Note: If there are two questions on a card, wait for the answer to the first before reading the second.

1. What is your attitude toward violence?

2. Do you think people are really good at heart? Are you?

3. What rights does a baby have? What rights does a fetus have?

4. How would you deal with a good friend you knew was getting deeply involved in drugs?

5. Tell about an event that happened in your family or in your own experience that you would call a miracle.

6. How do you react when you see a child being bullied? How do you act when the bully's victim is an unpopular teenager?

7. If you should parent a child before marriage, how much would you be willing to give up for the child?

8. Tell about a person (not a relative) that you can truly say is your brother or sister.

9. What do you believe happens to the human person after death?

10. How would you deal with a friend who is getting seriously drunk several times a week?

11. What are some of the things you can and should do to make your home a happier place?

12. What would you do if you found a wallet containing $500?

13. What would be your response to an invitation to spend your life as a priest, a sister, or a brother?

14. Explain to the group how you feel when you love someone.

15. On what basis do you select your same-sex friends? your opposite-sex friends?

16. Describe a true friend. How many friends do you have that fit that description?

17. What are your personal convictions about using marijuana and other drugs?

18. Name a person your age that you admire. Tell why.

19. What do you remember as the greatest day of your life?

20. Name one adult at school or at work whom you admire. Tell why.

21. Select a word or phrase that best describes your life at this time.

22. What person has most influenced your life? Try to tell how the person has affected you.

23. What change would you make in the church if you were the pope?

24. What is your greatest fear?

25. Name something that usually angers you and tell why. How do you react when you become angry?

26. When was the last time you really prayed about something? How was your prayer answered?

27. Select a word that you feel describes most people your age. Explain.

28. In school you have seen certain people all year and have seldom or never spoken to them. Explain why not.

29. What is the most difficult thing you have ever done?

30. When was the last time you cried and why?

31. What is the greatest value that guides your life?

32. What do you think people like in you the most? What about you do you think people might find annoying?

33. Share something that you like about your family. Share something that bugs you about them.

34. What was your best year in school? your worst year?

35. If you had to find a new name for God (a non-religious name), what word would you use?

36. Tell about a turning point in your life.

37. When do you feel most lonely? What do you do about it?

38. How would your parents react if you told them you wanted to enter full time ministry: priest, sister, brother, or lay minister?

39. Tell about a time when you lived up to your principles against pressure from the group. Tell about a time you gave in to pressure against your principles.

40. What do you consider really beautiful? really ugly?

41. Name a person whose advice, leadership, and concern for you seem to be completely trustworthy.

42. What earthly realties make you aware of Gods' presence? What causes you to doubt God's presence?

43. If your son or daughter told you they wanted to enter the ministry, how would you react?

44. Describe something in your life that you have always regretted doing or not doing.

45. Name a living person who is definitely improving the quality of life for the human race. How?

46. If both of your parents were killed suddenly in an accident and you were left on your own, how would your life be changed?

47. When are you most aware of and grateful for the gift of life?

48. If you knew a nuclear bomb was on its way, how would you spend your last thirty minutes?

49. Name three words that describe how your same-sex friends see you. Your opposite-sex friends.

50. What is the greatest crime one person can commit against another, not counting murder?

51. What do you consider your most prized material possession?

52. Describe what you *don't* want to be like as an adult.

53. Finish these statements: I feel most confident about myself when. . . . I feel least confident when. . . .

54. In what ways do you find yourself being a conformist and going along with the crowd?

76

55. What do you think are the biggest worries faced by today's male teenagers? female teenagers?

56. Where do you stand on the abortion question?

57. What are your views on stealing? How should society deter people your age from getting involved in stealing?

58. If you could have three wishes, what would you wish?

59. When was the last time you said the words "I love you" to your mother? to your father?

60. How would you respond to a person who brags to you about "having sex"?

61. What day in your life would you like to live over?

62. How important to you is honesty in dealing with your parents? your friends?

63. What do you think would be the best position in a family—oldest, youngest, or middle? How do you feel about where you are in your family?

64. What would you change about your family if you could?

65. What recent achievement are you proud of? Can you also name a recent failure?

66. Share three things that you are good at. How did you feel saying that to the group?

67. How do you feel about legalizing marijuana? Do you think we should have the same rules for marijuana as alcohol?

68. If you were the pope, what would you encourage the people of God to do?

69. What do you mean by the phrase "going steady"? What are the advantages and disadvantages of doing so?

70. Tell three words that best describe how your parents see you. How accurate are the words?

71. If your best friend were killed in an accident, how would you feel about God?

72. Is it more difficult in today's society to be a man or a to be a woman?

One-on-One Dialogues With Group Leaders

This can be a very beautiful experience for your group leaders as well as for the young people. It is a chance for each teenager to speak privately to an adult leader and a youth leader. (A youth leader is an older teen who has been trained for special leadership roles on the retreat or in the program.) A set of questions is provided for the leaders. These should be used merely as suggestions; the dialogue should be guided mainly by the interest and needs of each teen being spoken to.

Materials Needed:

▸ copies of the adult and youth leader directions (pages 79-80)

▸ copies of the Prayer for Peace (page 81) for each person (Give these to the youth leaders to give out to those who come to them for one-on-ones.)

Directions:

1. Arrange the room so each leader has a somewhat private space for the one-on-one dialogues. Set up each dialogue space with two chairs or beanbags and a lighted candle. Dim the lights.

2. Explain that the participants are free to approach any leader, not necessarily their table group leader. The conferences should last about five to ten minutes. If someone needs longer counseling for a specific problem, he or she should arrange another time for that with the leader.

3. Maintain an atmosphere of quiet reflection throughout the time of the conferences. Provide quiet activities that will keep everyone occupied.

4. If both adult and youth leaders are available, encourage the participants to have a conference with one of each.

One-on-One Dialogue—Adult Leaders

1. Begin the dialogue by greeting the young person by name. Encourage a bit of small talk to help him or her become comfortable.

2. Ask any of the questions below. Feel free to ask others based on the needs and interests of the person you are talking to.

Retreat

▶ How is the retreat going for you?
▶ How much of yourself are you putting into it?
▶ What did you expect it to be like?
▶ Which activities have you found the most helpful? difficult? boring? challenging?
▶ Would you want to go on a retreat again?

Confirmation Preparation (if applicable)

▶ What have you liked about your confirmation program? disliked?
▶ How have you cooperated?
▶ What have you been doing for service projects?
▶ How ready do you feel you are to be confirmed?
▶ Would you delay confirmation if you thought you were not ready?

Prayer

▶ Do you pray every day? when? where? how?
▶ Do you ever read the Bible on your own? Would you consider trying to do that regularly?
▶ What is your attitude toward Sunday Mass? Are you improving? Are you working at improving?

Family

▶ What is your attitude at home?
▶ How do you feel about your relationship with your mother? father? brothers and sisters?

▶ What would your parents like to see you improve in—besides grades?
▶ What could you do to make your family a happier place?

Reconciliation (if the sacrament is being offered)

▶ How do you feel about going to confession today?
▶ Do you have any questions about what to do or say? (If the person seems hesitant about going to confession, encourage him or her to use this chance to receive the sacrament of reconciliation.)

Vocation

▶ Do you know what you want to be when you "grow up"?
▶ Have you ever considered your vocation? Do you think you might be called to marriage? to the single life? to religious life?

3. Ask if there is anything else the young person would like to talk about.

4. Close with a short prayer and/or one of the following blessings:

May the Lord bless you and keep you.
May his face shine upon you and be gracious to you.
May he look upon you with kindness and give you his peace.

or

May the blessing of God rest upon you.
May his peace abide with you.
May his presence illuminate your heart, now and forevermore.

or

___Name___, I commend you to the Holy Spirit, through the most powerful intercession of the Blessed Virgin Mary, and I entrust you forever to her blessed hands.

One-on-One Dialogue—Youth Leaders

1. Greet your dialogue partner by name and make sure he or she is comfortable.

2. Ask some of the following questions, or any other questions you think would fit the person and the situation.

Retreat

▼ Have you ever been on a retreat before?

▼ How does this retreat compare to the other(s)? How is it different from what you may have expected?

▼ What did you like the best about what we've done so far? least?

▼ Would you consider coming back as a youth leader?

School

▼ How is school going this year?

▼ Do you have any favorite classes? any that you hate?

▼ What's the general attitude toward the teachers and administrators in your school?

▼ What's the drug-alcohol problem like at your school? Are you involved in any peer programs to try to help kids who have these problems?

▼ Does your school have a branch of SADD (Students Against Drunk Driving)? How effective is it?

Family

▼ Do you have older brothers and sisters? younger?

▼ How do you get along with everyone at home?

▼ Are your parents strict?

▼ What things do you like to do with your family?

Friends and Fun

▼ Who are your best friends right now? Tell me about them.

▼ Are cliques a problem in your school?

▼ How does your friendship group fit into the pecking order?

▼ What do you usually do for fun?

▼ Are you into sports? music? plays? parties?

Parish

▼ How active are you in your parish youth group?

▼ Are you involved with anything church?

▼ Does your parish offer Masses that are geared to youth?

Work

▼ Do you have a job? How many hours?

▼ Do you like your job? What is your boss like?

▼ Is this the kind of work you would like to do for a living?

▼ Do you find it hard to keep up with all your commitments—work, school, church, friends, family?

3. Close this dialogue by reciting together the Prayer of St. Francis (page 81).

prayer for peace

Lord, make me an instrument of peace:

where there is hatred, let me sow love;

where there is injury, pardon;

where there is doubt, faith;

where there is despair, hope;

where there is darkness, light;

and where there is sadness, joy.

O Divine Master,

grant that I may not so much seek

to be consoled as to console;

to be understood as to understand;

to be loved as to love;

for it is in giving that we receive;

it is in pardoning that we are pardoned;

and it is in dying that we

are born to eternal life.

—attributed to St. Francis

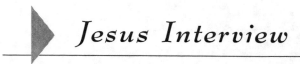

Jesus Interview

Materials and Preparation Needed:

▸ copies of the twelve questions on pages 83-84 (Cut them apart. You will need two or three questions for each person in your class.)

▸ a volunteer (youth or adult) to "play Jesus" in the upcoming interview

▸ a microphone (even a fake microphone will do)

Directions:

1. Gather everyone in the large-group area. Say:

   Yesterday I received a phone call from radio station HVEN. They are sending over a celebrity to interview some of us for a special on tonight's news. Most of you have probably heard of the celebrity, his formal name is Jesus Christ, but his friends call him J.C. The station wants us to be well-prepared for the interview so they've sent over a set of questions like those he'll probably ask (*Give everyone two or three questions.*) I'm giving each of you some of the questions to prepare. Spend the next twenty minutes or so thinking about your questions and jotting down things you might say to answer them. You may work with a partner if you wish.

2. Bring in "Jesus" with his microphone. Have Jesus walk among the group talk-show host style, asking questions like those the students have reflected on.

Do you think your religion classes have helped or hindered your love for me?

What do you think about my church? Do you think it's going the way I planned? How would you suggest it be improved?

Are you afraid to die? What do you think I meant when I said, "Those who believe in me will never die?"

What do you think is the biggest problem in the world? Is there something you think I should do about it? What are *you* doing to solve it?

How well do you know my Father? Have my followers done a good job of telling you about him?

What would you like me to do for your family? for you? for your friends?

83

Do you know anyone who truly lives the way I expect people to live? Tell me about him or her. Would you like to live that way? What seems to be the biggest obstacle for you?

May I come to your house for dinner? How will you introduce me? Do you think the dinner conversation will be different because I am there?

May I spend the whole day with you tomorrow? How do you think the day will go with me along? How would you explain me to your friends?

Are you usually happy? What do you need to make you happier than you are? Is there anything that could make you perfectly happy? Can I help?

Would you like to be my friend? I seem to have trouble making friends in your school. What do you think my problem is?

My church needs dynamic, prayerful leaders, but I seem to be having trouble recruiting people your age these days. What do you think I should do to encourage you and your peers to work for me?

84

God Questions

This is an excellent exercise to use with a mixed group of youth and adults, for example, a parent-youth retreat. It can also be used in many other settings.

Materials and Preparations Needed:

▸ copies of the "God Questions" handout (page 87)

▸ Set up chairs for half the group in a circle around the outside of the large-group area. Set up another circle of chairs facing them.

▸ For the follow-up activity, you will need a small-group area.

Directions:

1. Ask all the girls to sit on the outside chairs, facing a boy, and all the boys to sit on the inside chairs, facing a girl. (*Use the adults in either the inside or outside chairs to even off the sets.*) Say:

   One way we can realize how much we've grown in our faith understanding is to remember how we thought about things when we were little children. So dig back into your memory bank now and tell your partner what you thought God looked like when you were a little child. The outside person answers first, then the inside person. (*Allow time for both answers.*)

2. After the discussion is finished, present the following questions for discussion, using the same procedure as before:

   How has your idea of God changed? What kind of mental image do you use for God now? Do you think of God in human form? Do you have separate images for Jesus and for God the Father? (*Allow time for answers.*)

3. Instruct everyone in the outside circle to stand and move three chairs to the right. (*Wait until all are relocated.*) Say:

   Tell your new partner what the "little-kid you" thought God's job was. What did you think God did all day up there in heaven? This time the inside person answers first. (*Allow time for answers.*)

4. Continue. Say:

   And now what do you think God's job is? What role does God play in human life? When we pray for people who are sick, does God make them better? Does he give the farmers rain when they pray for it? When Notre Dame plays USC and both teams are praying to win, does God choose sides? (*Allow time for answers.*)

5. Say:

Now it's the inside circles turn to move three chairs to the right. (*Continue in this manner for each of the following sets of questions. Always ask a THEN question and allow time for the answers, then ask a NOW question.*)

THEN Questions

Tell your partner about your childhood ideas of right and wrong. How did you know good from bad? What kind of discipline did your parents use? Was it effective?

Describe for your partner your childhood ideas of heaven and hell.

When you were a child what prayers did you say? Did you pray as a family? What's your earliest memory of really praying for something?

NOW Questions

Where do you look for moral guidance in your life today? Do you still follow your parents' moral teachings? Should you? In your opinion, are most people basically good or basically evil?

What do you believe now about life after death? How do you understand heaven and hell? Do you plan on going to heaven someday? Do you know anyone who you are sure is in heaven? in hell?

How do you pray now? When and where? Do you pray formula prayers or do you use your own words? Do you have a sense of God's presence when you pray? Do you think he really listens and cares?

6. When all are finished, have everyone return to their dialogue tables. Give everyone a copy of the God Questions handout. Say:

This paper contains a list of questions like those we were just dealing with. Read the questions through silently and mark with an "X" any question that is of special interest to you. (*Allow time.*)

7. Continue. Say:

Take turns around the circle. When it is your turn, select one of your marked questions. Ask whether anyone else also has that area marked. Then spend some time as a table discussing the question. If you come upon a problem and would like it to be brought up in the entire group, let me know when I come around.

8. Circulate among the tables. If any table wants a question brought to the large group, do that at the end of the discussion time or set another time if there are many questions.

GOD QUESTIONS

____What kind of mental image do you use for God?

____Do you think of God in human form?

____Do you have separate images for Jesus and for God the Father?

____What role does God play in human life?

____When we pray for people who are sick, does God make them better?

____Does God give farmers rain when they pray for it?

____When two teams are playing a game and both teams are praying to win, does God choose sides?

____Are most people basically good or basically evil?

____Where do you look for moral guidance in your life?

____Do you still follow your parents' moral teachings? Should you?

____What is the best way to train children to be good moral persons?

____What do you believe about life after death?

____How do you understand heaven and hell?

____Do you plan on going to heaven someday?

____Do you know anyone who you are sure is now in heaven?

____How do you pray?

____When and where do you pray?

____Is it better to pray formula prayers or to use your own words?

____Do you have a sense of God's presence when you pray?

____Do you think God really listens and cares?

▶ *Jesus' Feelings*

Materials Needed:

- ▶ bibles

- ▶ copies of the Jesus' Feelings (page 89) handout

- ▶ pencils or pens

- ▶ background music and something to play it on

Directions:

1. Distribute bibles and copies of the "Jesus' Feelings" handout. Say:

   When I finish giving these directions, I would like you all to move to a spot in this room where you can be on an "island" alone. Then select any passage on this paper that interests you. Read the passage slowly and try to imagine what Jesus must be feeling in that event. Try to get inside Jesus' skin and feel the situation with him. Then write on your paper a short prayer to Jesus telling him your feelings about that event.

2. When all the participants are settled in their alone spots, play some gentle background music. You may have to walk around the room helping people to find the passage they wish to read. Allow about 30 minutes, then say:

   Move near someone now and share with the person one of the passages you chose. Talk about Jesus' feelings and yours as you reflected on that passage. If you have time, share a second passage.

3. After the sharing time, say:

   Now move back to your alone spot. Put your hands quietly on your lap and close your eyes.

4. When a quiet peace has settled over the room play some background music to set the mood. Then pray:

   Jesus, we thank you for the gift of human feelings. We thank you for becoming human and experiencing the same feelings with us. When we have feelings that are hard to deal with, help us to look to you to see how you would have handled them. We offer to you our fears, our angers, our sadness, and our frustrations. We also want to share with you all our joys, our hopefulness, our courage, and our love. Help us to be sensitive to the feelings of others just as we want them to be to ours. Thank you, again, Jesus, for your humanity and our own. Amen.

Jesus' Feelings

Did Jesus have feelings? If he did how do his feelings compare to mine?

Scripture tells us that Jesus was like us in all things except sin. He must have experienced human emotions very similar to ours. Explore the New Testament to see how many of our own emotions Jesus really experienced and how he coped with them.

1. Jesus was angry. (Mk 11:15ff; Mt 23:13ff)

2. Jesus showed fear. (Mt 26:36-38)

3. Jesus was happy and could celebrate. (Jn 2:1-11; Lk 10:21)

4. Jesus experienced frustration. (Mt 23:37ff)

5. Jesus experienced personal hunger and was aware that others were hungry. (Mt 4:1-2; Jn 6:1-7; Jn 4:4-8, 31-34; Lk 6:1-5)

6. Jesus cried. (Jn 11:32-38; Lk 19:41)

7. Jesus was impatient. (Jn 14:8ff; Mk 10:35-45)

8. Jesus felt sympathy for others. (Lk 4:38ff; Mt 20:29-34; Mt 14:14; Mt 9:35ff)

9. Jesus was merciful. (Lk 23:39-43)

10. Jesus forgave and considered forgiveness important. (Lk 23:34; Lk 6:27-37; Lk 7:37-50; Mt 18:21-22; Mt 6:12-15; Mk 3:28)

My prayer:

PRAYERS

Words for the Heart

Materials and Preparations Needed:

- ▸ a copy of the "Prayer Starters" handout (page 95) for each participant. Cut the sheets apart and assemble the starters so that each person receives one complete set.

- ▸ a bible for each participant

- ▸ pencils and lap pads

- ▸ appropriate background music

Directions:

1. Gather in dialogue groups. You will also need enough space for the participants to move to "alone" spots later.

2. Give everyone a bible and set of prayer starters. Say:

   Work together to find the ten passages in the bible. Use the prayer starters as bookmarks. Don't read the passages yet.

3. When all the bibles are marked say:

   Now take your bible and move to a corner of this room where you can be "alone." Be sure you are at least six feet away from everyone else and on the other side of the room from anyone who might distract you from prayer.

4. When all are settled and quiet, say:

   Hold your bible in your hands and think about what it is that you are holding. This holy book has been reverenced by Jews and Christians for thousands of years. In it we find the story of God's love for his chosen people. If we read this book with faith, it is possible for God to speak directly to our hearts through the words on these pages. But we must come to the reading with our hearts open and ready to hear God speaking.

   Your bible is marked now with ten special passages, any or all of which might have a message for you today. When I finish giving these directions, open to any one of them, read the passage over several times, and ask God to tell you what he wants you to hear in those words. Spend some time just talking with God about the meaning of the passage, then write his message to you on the slip of paper. It isn't necessary to complete all ten passages. You could even spend the whole prayer period dialoguing with God about just one or two. Before you begin, spend a few minutes just holding the book lovingly in your hands as you would hold a letter from a dear friend. Ask God to open your mind and heart to his word. When your heart is ready, turn to one of the passages and begin.

5. Play some quiet music as a background to the scripture prayer. Allow thirty to forty-five minutes depending on the prayerfulness of the group. Toward the end of the prayer period say:

Look back over all the passages you have prayed about, and select one or two favorites that you would be willing to share with your small group. (*Allow a few more minutes for this.*)

6. Ask everyone to meet in dialogue groups, then say:

Take turns sharing your favorite passages. Explain to your group what personal message those words of scripture held for you today. Each person share one passage; if there is time, share another.

PRAYER STARTERS

Dt 6:4-9	Jn 6:35-40
Mt 6:5-14	Is 58:5-11
Ps 62:6-12	Eph 4:1-6
Lk 12:22-31	Jer 29:11-13
Prv 3:21-31	2 Tm 1:6-8

In Touch With God

Most young people have had little previous experience with retreats. This talk and prayer is very suitable for a retreat opening. It sets the tone of seriousness and prayerfulness for the rest of the retreat.

Materials Needed:

▶ a recording of a contemporary Christian song with lyrics that speak of our deepening relationship with God

▶ a large candle

Directions:

1. Arrange cushions or pillows in a large informal circle in the large-group area. Invite the retreatants to join you in the prayer circle. Place a lighted candle in the center of the circle, dim the lights, and give a short talk based on the following script.

Script

A retreat is a very special time. We step out of the everyday routines of our lives and into a whole new way of thinking and acting. This is definitely not what you're usually doing at this time on this day of the week. You're in a different place, with different people, and doing very different things than you normally would.

What happens during a retreat?

The main thing we do is spend time getting in touch with our own hearts. We ask ourselves: Who am I? Who is this person who lives inside my skin? What's important to me? Whom do I love? What do I really want out of life? We try to get past the masks that we so often hide behind and discover what's going on in our deepest, truest hearts.

And when we get quiet enough and serious enough to pay attention to our hearts, we usually discover that God is living there. Even if we haven't been paying much attention to him, God is there, waiting for us to notice him, wanting us to love him the way he loves us.

Another thing that happens when we listen to our hearts is that we often find out that there are things about the way we've been living that we're not very pleased with. The deepest, truest part of us knows what's right and what's wrong. During a retreat we often discover things about our own lives that we want to change.

I'd like you to listen prayerfully now to the words of this song, encouraging us and drawing us to a deeper relationship with God. (*Play the song you have chosen.*)

2. After the song, say:

Close your eyes now and spend a few minutes talking to God who lives in the deepest part of you. Tell him how you feel about being on this retreat (*Pause.*) Thank God for giving you life, and for giving his life for you. (*Pause.*) Offer him your deepest heart during this time of retreat and ask him to open it to his love. (*Pause.*) Amen.

Luke 19
(Meditation)

Meditation is an ancient and revered form of prayer. Every era of the Christian tradition has known men and women from all walks of life for whom meditative prayer was a powerful means of coming close to God and the inner mysteries of human life. Contemporary society has recently rediscovered the power of meditation to heal the human spirit. You may be surprised to find how responsive young people are to meditation experiences like this one.

Materials Needed:

▸ copies of the "Luke 19" handout (page 101)

▸ pencils or pens

▸ lap pads

▸ bible

Directions

1. Explain to the participants that they will be moving to "alone" spots for the next meditation experience. If the room is carpeted, invite them to lie on their backs on the floor. If not, tell them to sit on the floor or on a straight-back chair. To meditate well, the spine should be kept very straight, the body relaxed but alert. They should take with them the "Luke 19" handout, a pencil, and a lap pad. When all are settled, say:

    Stretch your legs out straight and rest your hands comfortably on the floor beside you (*Or*: Put your feet flat on the floor and rest your hands comfortably on your lap.) Now tense all the muscles in your body. Hold the tension for a moment, then relax. Close your eyes. Breathe in deeply through your nostrils, count to four, then blow your breath out through your mouth with a slight wooshing sound. Let's do that together five times. In two-three-four. Out-two-three-four. (*Expect a little silliness here, but call for respectful quiet before continuing.*)

    Now keep your entire body as quiet as possible, and your mind and heart as alert as possible as you take an imaginary walk with me.

2. Present a meditation based on the following script:

Script

It's a beautiful spring (or fall or winter) day, and you are walking home from school alone. You're busy mulling over all that has happened in school today—the kids you talked to, the fun you had at lunch, maybe the trouble you were in. You're so deep in thought that you hardly hear your name being called. The person calls again gently. You turn around and coming toward you is a tall stranger. You're not at all afraid, and you wonder why not after all the warnings you've heard about strangers. But when you look again, you realize that this man isn't really a stranger. You don't know how you know, but you are sure the man walking you home from school is Jesus.

He puts his arm around your shoulder and gives you a little squeeze, and says "Hi, Bill" (or Patti or Mary Jo). What do you say in response? Imagine the conversation you and Jesus would have as you walk along toward home. He starts it off by asking you how school went today. Talk to him in your imagination about your classes, your friends, your school problems. (*Allow two or three minutes of silence. During this time carry on an imaginary conversation with Jesus in your own mind.*)

You're standing in front of your house now. You don't know just what to do with Jesus, so you invite him to come in. You open the door, wondering what your mom will say when she sees the stranger you brought home. You say, "Hi, Mom," and are about to explain about Jesus, but he puts his finger on his lips and winks. And then you realize that your mom doesn't see him. He's only visible to you. Think of the way you usually act when you get home from school. Would you treat your family any differently if your were conscious that Jesus was watching and listening? Take time now to talk to Jesus about your family. Mention each member of the family by name and tell Jesus about your relationship with each one. (*Pause for reflection.*)

You invite Jesus into your room. He comes in and looks all around. How do you feel about your space with Jesus in it? Talk to him about your personal treasures—the pictures on the wall, the things in your dresser and on the shelves, your favorite CDs, the award you won in fourth grade. Is there anything in your room you'd rather Jesus didn't see? Since you know he can see everything anyway, talk to him about the parts of your life that you might be embarrassed by or ashamed of as well as those parts that you are pleased with and proud of. (*Pause for reflection.*)

Jesus is sitting on your bed now, leafing through your school yearbook. Talk to him about your friends. In your imagination, introduce them to him one by one. Tell him what you find special about each one, and what you think each one needs from Jesus. If you have a special girlfriend or boyfriend, be sure to talk to Jesus about that relationship. If you don't have a special someone in your life right now, tell Jesus honestly how you feel about that. Is it a problem for you? Take time now to talk to Jesus about each of your friends. (*Pause for reflection.*)

Jesus stands, and you can tell that he is getting ready to leave. He puts his hand on your shoulder and looks at you tenderly. "You are very special to me," he says. Feel his hand on your shoulder. See his eyes smiling at you. Hear him say these words to you: "You are very special to me, Bill" (Patti, Mary Jo). (*Pause.*) Tell him how you liked spending this time with him. (*Pause.*) He asks you if you'll spend time like this with him everyday. Can you promise him you will? Set a definite time and place. (*Pause.*)

You walk Jesus to the door and watch him as he walks briskly down the sidewalk. He turns at the corner and waves. Keep watching him till he's too far away to see. Then open your eyes and sit up quietly.

3. Read aloud the story of Zacchaeus from Luke 19:1-7 and the introduction at the top of the "Luke 19" handout. Ask the participants to work the exercise, using just words or phrases.

4. After they have finished, have the participants meet in dialogue groups. When the groups have formed, say:

Take one round to tell your table how the meditation experience went for you. Could you imagine Jesus in your home? Could you really "hear" him talking to you? Did anything distract you? Did you just fall asleep? In a second round, share one thing from your reflection sheet that you are willing to talk about with your group.

LUKE 19

Imagine that, like Zacchaeus, Jesus comes to your house. He spends about a week with you, your family, and your friends. In your mind, walk through the events and situations of a typical week. The presence of Jesus might cause you to see some things about everyday places and people that you sometimes fail to see. Imagine what Jesus would be pleased to see happening in your family, among your friends, at your school or work. Hear what Jesus would say is displeasing to him.

Jesus says:

"I am pleased with

Jesus says:

"I am displeased with

YOUR FAMILY
because

YOUR FRIENDS
because

YOUR SCHOOL OR WORK PLACE
because

YOU
because

God's Promises and Mine

This prayer can be used in connection with the "Promises and Commitment" presentation and response, pages 29-32.

Materials Needed:

▶ copies of "God's Promises to Me" handout (page 103)

Directions:

1. Gather the participants in a large group. Say:

    Faith and religion depend very much on promises and commitments. The scriptures tell us many times that God's relationship with his people is based on a covenant, a promise. The covenant with God is a two-way promise. God says to us, "I will be your God and you will be my people." God promises he will be a loving, protecting, providing God. And, in return, he wants us to be a caring, obedient, loving people.

    Faith, then, is an interchange of promises. God promises us his love, and we promise him our love. We know for sure that we can rely on God to be true to his promise. Can he be as sure of us?

    Growing in faith means two things: growing in our belief in God's half of the covenant, and growing in our commitment to our half. As our faith grows, we come to a deeper realization that we can always count on God to be true to us. We learn to rely on his love, to depend on him to care for us and for our loved ones. At the same time, growth in faith means deepening our commitment to God, growing in our willingness to make promises to God and to live up to them. As we mature in faith, we become persons God can depend on to help create a loving, caring world based on his plan for creation.

2. Pass out copies of "God's Promises to Me" and say:

    On this sheet you will find several passages from the Bible. Some of the passages are the words of God speaking a promise to his people. Some remind us of how faithful God is in keeping his promises. We are going to spend some quiet time now meditating on God's promises and what they say to our heart. Find a quiet spot where you can be "alone," and read the passages slowly, one at a time. Try to hear God speaking the words directly to you. Tune in to what God is saying in your heart through the words of scripture. Don't necessarily try to finish all the passages. You might spend the whole prayer time with just two or three. (*Allow 20 to 30 minutes.*)

3. Say:

    Mark the one passage that names the promise you most need to hear from God today. Then write your responding promise to God in the space provided. (*Allow time.*)

God's promises to me:

He whose name is the Lord said, "Call to me, and I will answer you; I will tell you wonderful and marvelous things that you know nothing about" (Jer 33:2-3).

And so I am sure that God who began this good work in you will carry it on until it is finished on the Day of Christ Jesus (Phil 1:6).

And God is able to give you more than you need, so that you will always have all you need for yourselves and more than enough for every good cause (2 Cor 9:8).

I have the strength to face all conditions by the power that Christ gives me (Phil 4:13).

We know that in all things God works for good with those who love him, those whom he has called according to his purpose (Ro 8:28).

But those who trust in the Lord for help
will find their strength renewed.
They will rise on wings like eagles;
they will run and not get weary;
they will walk and not grow weak (Is 40:31).

Ask, and you will receive; seek, and you will find; knock, and the door will be opened to you. For everyone who asks will receive, and anyone who seeks will find, and the door will be opened to those who knock (Mt 7:7-8).

Every test that you have experienced is the kind that normally comes to people. But God keeps his promise, and he will not allow you to be tested beyond your power to remain firm; at the time you are put to the test, he will give you the strength to endure it, and so provide you with a way out (1 Cor 10:13).

"Listen! I stand at the door and knock; if any hear my voice and open the door, I will come into their house and eat with them, and they will eat with me" (Rev 3:20).

Who, then, can separate us from the love of Christ? Can trouble do it, or hardship or persecution or hunger or poverty or danger or death? . . . No, in all these things we have complete victory through him who loved us! For I am certain that nothing can separate us from his love: neither death nor life, neither angels nor other heavenly rulers or powers, neither the present nor the future, neither the world above nor the world below—there is nothing in all creation that will ever be able to separate us from the love of God which is ours through Christ Jesus our Lord (Ro 8:35-39).

And I will always guide you and satisfy you with good things. I will keep you strong and well. You will be like a garden that has plenty of water, like a spring of water that never goes dry (Is 58:11).

"I will ask the Father, and he will give you another Helper, who will stay with your forever. He is the Spirit, who reveals the truth about God" (Jn 14:16).

"Those who love me will obey my teaching. My Father will love them, and my Father and I will come to them and live with them" (Jn 14:23).

"Go, then, to all peoples everywhere and make them my disciples: baptize them in the name of the Father, the Son, and the Holy Spirit, and teach them to obey everything I have commanded you. And I will be with you always, to the end of the age" (Mt 28:19-20).

My promises to God:

The Blind See

This prayer can be used in connection with the "Trust Walk" community building exercise, pages 50-52.

Materials and Preparation Needed:

▶ three bibles (mark one at Mt 9:27-30, the second at Mk 8:22-25, the third at Lk 18:35-43)

▶ three volunteer readers for the prayer experience

▶ several adult leaders to touch the "blind" students

▶ recording of instrumental or appropriate-themed music with lyrics

▶ copies of "A Hymn of Praise" handout (page 105)

Directions:

1. Gather in a chapel or prayer room. Pass out copies of "A Hymn of Praise" handout to each participant. Say:

   Close your eyes and sit quietly for a few moment. Imagine that you are blind. Try to put yourself back into the time of Jesus and think what it would have been like to have him cure you of your blindness. Keep your eyes closed while you listen to these scriptural accounts of Jesus curing the blind man.

2. Call on the volunteers to read the Bible readings, one at a time. (*Allow some quiet time after each reading.*)

   After all the readings are finished, say:

   Keep your eyes closed. Hear Jesus saying now in your heart, "What do you want me to do for you?" Answer him. What do you need from him? Maybe you have a blindness that needs healing, a blindness that keeps you from believing and trusting in God, from seeing your own goodness, from finding a way out of a problem you are entangled in. (*Pause.*)

   In the reading from Mark the blind man was brought to Jesus by his friends. Maybe you, too, have friends or family members who need Jesus to touch them. Maybe people you love are being blinded by anger, jealousy, selfishness, alcohol, or some other problem. Bring them to Jesus. Ask him to touch the blind spot in their lives and heal them. (*Pause.*)

   The leaders and I will now walk among you, touching each of you with the healing touch of Jesus. When you have been touched, open your eyes while remaining quiet. (*Walk among the group, prayerfully touching each person on the shoulder for a few moments. As you do this, play music you have chosen.*)

3. After the song, say:

   In each of the scriptural stories, those who had been healed praised God for the new gift of sight. Let us now praise him together. The words of Psalm 100 are on your handout sheet.

A Hymn of Praise

Sing to the Lord, all the world!

Worship the Lord with joy;

　　come before him with happy songs!

Acknowledge that the Lord is God.

　　He made us and we belong to him;

　　we are his people, we are his flock.

Enter the Temple gates with thanksgiving;

　　go into its courts with praise.

　　Give thanks to him and praise him.

The Lord is good;

　　his love is eternal

　　and his faithfulness lasts forever

—Ps 100

Here I Am, Lord

This prayer works very well as a closing prayer on the first night of a retreat. It can also be adapted for use at other times.

Materials Needed:

▶ a recording or lyrics for "Here I Am, Lord" by Dan Schutte

▶ lap pads

▶ copies of the "Here I Am, Lord" handout (page 107)

▶ a candle (lit before the group gathers) for each dialogue group

Directions:

1. Gather in the large-group area. Later the group will break into small groups and go to their "cozy corner" areas.

2. Invite the group to sit in a prayer circle. Pass out copies of the "Here I Am, Lord" handout, lap pads, and pencils. Say:

   The song we are going to play (or sing) is like a dialogue with Jesus. He speaks the verses and we respond with the chorus. In the song Jesus calls each of us to open our hearts to his people, to care for those who are hurting, those who are lonely, those who are in any kind of need. "Whom can I send," Jesus asks, "to heal my broken world?" Can you respond, "Here I am, Lord. Send me"?

   As you are listening to the song, write in the heart the names of all the people you hold in your heart, and the people you should hold there. As you write each name silently say to Jesus, "Here I am, Lord. Help me to love this person the way you want me to."

3. Play "Here I Am, Lord." After the song, say:

   You will be moving to cozy corners for the closing part of this prayer. Group leaders, please take one of the lighted candles with you. When you get to your corner, form a close circle sitting on the floor. Then, pass the candle around the circle twice. The first time the candle is passed, each person will tell the group three things: how you felt about this retreat before you came; how you feel about it now; and what you hope will happen in your heart because you are here. The second time, pass the candle in silence. This time, each person is to hold the candle for a few moments while everyone else prays silently for him or her. When everyone has been prayed for, put the candle in the center of your group. Each person is to reach out and touch the base of the candle with one hand. Then pray the Our Father together remembering that Jesus promised to be with us whenever we gather in his name.

Here I am, Lord

Then I heard the Lord say,

"Whom shall I send?

Who will be our messenger?"

I answered,

"I will go! Send me!"

I will hold your people in my heart

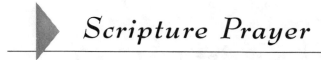

Scripture Prayer

Materials and Preparation Needed:

▸ copies of the "Scripture Prayer" handout (page 110); cut the sheets apart and assemble the starters so each person receives one complete set.

▸ a bible for each participant

▸ a recording of background music

Directions:

1. Have everyone gather in the large-group area. Give everyone a bible and a set of "Scripture Prayer" starters. Say:

Work together to find these ten passages in the New Testament. Use the prayer starters as bookmarks. Don't read the passages yet.

2. When all the bibles are marked, say:

Now take your bibles and move to a corner of this room where you can be alone. Be sure you are at least six feet away from anyone else and on the other side of the room from your best friend.

3. When all are settled and quiet, give a talk based on the following script.

Script

Open your books to the New Testament. What you are looking at now is a link to the historical person, Jesus of Nazareth. The words in front of you were reported by people who knew Jesus personally, people who saw his miracles, who heard his teachings, who stood under his cross, who touched with their own hands his risen body.

We who live now in the post-Eater time, the time when Jesus lives in the world through us, can come to know Jesus better by lovingly and prayerfully reading these words. When we read the New Testament with faith, it is often possible to experience Jesus speaking directly to our own hearts through the words of scripture.

Today, we are going to try to experience that living word. When I finish giving the directions, turn to any passage you have marked. Read the passage several times, prayerfully and attentively. Spend some time talking to Jesus about the passage, asking him to tell you what message he wants you to hear in those words. Write his message to you on the marker, and then turn to another passage. It isn't necessary to do all ten passages. Spend as much time as you can talking with Jesus about any of them.

Quiet your heart now. Ask Jesus to speak to you through the words of his gospel. When your heart is ready, open the bible and begin. (*Play some quiet music as a background to the scripture prayer. Allow 30 to 45 minutes, depending on the prayerfulness of the group.*)

4. Toward the end of the prayer period, say:

Look back over all the passages you have prayed over and select one or two favorites to share with your small group.

5. Gather in dialogue groups. Say:

Take turns sharing your favorite passage. Explain to your group what personal message those words of scripture held for you today.

Scripture Prayer

MATTHEW 5:13-16

MARK 9:33-41

LUKE 6:43-45

JOHN 10:11-16

1 CORINTHIANS 9:24-27

MATTHEW 9:9-12

MARK 11:22-25

LUKE 12:22-31

JOHN 15:1-4

EPHESIANS 3:14-21

Letters to God, Letters From God

Materials and Preparation Needed:

- lap pads
- pencils
- a recording of background music
- copies of "Letter-to-God" and "Letter-from-God" stationery (page 113)

Directions:

1. Gather in a large group to pass out the materials and give instructions. First give everyone a copy of the Letter-to-God stationery, a lap pad, and pencil. Then say:

   Sometimes when we find it difficult to keep our minds on prayer, it helps to write our thoughts to God in the form of a letter. Take this paper now and move to a corner of the room where you can be alone. When you are settled, spend the first few minutes just getting in touch with the presence of God within you. Then begin to write. Use the sentence starters around the edge of the paper for ideas. Try to write at least one paragraph about each idea. What you write in your letter will be between you and God only; you will not be asked to share it. When you have finished, come to me or another group leader and we will give you your next activity.

2. Play some background music softly as the group is writing. When individuals approach you for the second activity, give them the Letter-from-God stationery and say:

   On this paper you are going to write God's answer to your letter. First spend some time thinking about these words from the prophet Isaiah. God is speaking to you and saying: "Do not be afraid. You are mine and I love you." Try to really *hear* God saying that to you tonight. Think. What else does God want to say to me? How would he answer the letter I just wrote him? Then write "Dear (*your name*)" on your paper and write a letter from God to you.

Alternate Directions:

1. Tell the group to sign their Letter-to-God anonymously, for example, Troubled in Wisconsin, A Lonely Left-out, Happy to be Alive. Explain that later their letter will be given to someone in the group to answer in God's name. They will have to remember how they signed their letter so they will know which answer to claim.

2. Collect all the letters, then give them out again. Make sure no one gets his or her own letter. Give everyone a piece of Letter-from-God stationery and an envelope. Say:

Reverently read the letter you now have, remembering it was written to God. Then spend some time praying for the person whose letter you just read. Ask God to let you know what he wants the person to hear from him tonight. Then answer the letter in God's name. When you have finished, put both letters in the envelope, address it to the original writer, seal it, and give it to me.

3. Collect all the letters and give them out at an appropriate time. You may wish to have the letters remain unsealed so that you can check them for appropriateness before returning them to the original writer.

"I have called you by name - you are mine. When you pass through deep waters, I will be with you! Your troubles will not overwhelm you ... You are precious to me ...

"Be not afraid - I will save you. ...

Do not be afraid - I am with you!" (Is 43:1-5).

Dear God, Life really confuses me sometimes ... I wish you would help me with ... you say that you love me, but ... I have a problem with ... you've given me much to be grateful for ... what would really make me happy is ... Please forgive me for ... I promise ...

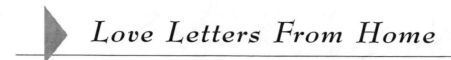

Love Letters From Home

Materials and Preparation Needed:

▸ a letter for each teenager

  About three or four weeks before the retreat, send the parents a letter (see sample on page 116) explaining the love letter idea and its importance. Tell the parents that the letters should be kept secret. Have the letters returned to you well before the retreat.

  Check the letters against your list as they arrive. Make *sure* you get one for everyone. If you do not, don't plan on this activity. Instead, give out the letters that you have received *privately* toward the end of the retreat and ask the participants to read them at home.

▸ stationery, envelopes, and a candle in a glass holder for each group. Have the leaders pick these up along with the letters for their groups.

▸ a recording of a song with lyrics that speak of the kind of deep, caring love parents have for their children

Directions:

1. Have the participants gather in the prayer space with each small group sitting together in a circle on the floor. The area should be large enough for the participants to move to "alone" spots to read and respond to their letters.

2. Have the leaders put the lighted candle and the letters in the center of their circle. Put the letters face down so the names don't show. Say:

   Our God is a loving God, but most of us have a hard time learning to believe that. We're not sure that he loves us. The best way God has of teaching us about his love for us is through the loving people he sends into our lives. And for most of us, the most loving people of all are our parents.

   I'd like you to spend a moment thinking of all the loving your parents have given you over the years. Draw pictures in your memory: your mom hugging you when you were hurt or afraid; your dad carrying you on his shoulders; sitting in your dad's lap as he read you a book; running in after school to tell your mom you won your first game. See if you can remember yourself being loved at each stage of your growing up. (*Pause.*)

   I am going to play a song with lyrics that speak of love and care. (*Add more detail according to the song you have chosen.*) As you listen to the song, imagine the words being spoken to you concerning the love your parents and God have for you.

3. After the song, say:

> Our parents are the first to teach us about love, but they are often the hardest people for us to learn to love well. Tonight we have a special gift for you—a love letter from your parents. Your group leaders will give out the letters and some stationery and envelopes. Go off by yourself to read your letters and to answer them. When you're finished, seal your answer, address it, and hand it in. We'll stamp the letters and mail them.

4. Play the song again as the letters are being distributed.

Alternative:

> It is possible—and valuable—to have the young people write a letter to their parents even if you did not do the letters-from-parents part of this exercise. It will require more motivation, however.

Sample Letter to Parents

Dear Parents,

I am writing to ask for your help in a very special part of the retreat your son/daughter will be attending (*date of your retreat*). I would like you to write a "love letter" to your child, telling him/her about the deep love you feel.

In our busy and hectic lives we often forget to say the most important things to the people who mean the most to us. Please take this opportunity to tell your son/daughter all the special things you love about her/him, to share your favorite memories of your teen's childhood, to express your loving hope for his/her future, etc.

You may write just one letter signed by either or both parents, or each parent may write a separate letter; that is up to you. However, it is very important that every teen on the retreat have a letter. If I do not receive a letter for *everyone*, I will have to replace this retreat activity with something else. Send your letter in an envelope with your child's name on it and mail it to *me* in an outer envelope.

Please get your letter to me by (*date at least two weeks before the retreat*) so that I can be certain I will be able to do this activity. The love letters are to be a surprise so please do not mention the letter to your son/daughter ahead of time.

Thank you.

Be Not Afraid
(Night Prayer)

This prayer experience helps teens to face some of the many fears that linger in their hearts, and to turn trustfully to God for strength and control.

Materials Needed:

▶ lyrics and/or recording of "Be Not Afraid" by Robert Dufford, SJ (New Dawn Music)

▶ one lighted candle for each discussion group

Directions:

1. Present a meditation based on the following script. Talk from behind the group, in a quiet meditative tone of voice.

Script

Take a moment to quiet your body, your mind, your heart. (*Pause.*) Tonight we're going to spend a few minutes getting in touch with an emotion none of us likes to experience—fear. We are all afraid sometimes. Even though we don't usually admit it, fear plays a big part in most of our lives. The fears of adults differ from those of teens, the fears of teens differ from those of children, but everybody has fears. Sometimes our fears are quiet and subtle, and we are hardly aware that they are influencing us. At other times fear is so strong in us that it paralyzes us and we can't act or think rationally.

What are your personal fears? Are you aware of them? Can you name them?

Maybe you're secretly afraid that your friends don't really like you, that they talk about you behind your back. Most of us have that kind of fear sometimes, even though we seldom admit it to anyone. Psychologists call it the fear of abandonment.

Maybe it's the future that frightens you. School seems to be getting tougher and there's a class you're afraid you might not pass. Or you're afraid of not making the football team or not being selected for the play or not succeeding in the scholarship exam. Do you worry about college? your job? your future careers?

Some of you have home problems that cause you fear. You might be afraid to open the door of your own house after school because you fear a confrontation with your parents. Maybe you've lied to them, and you're afraid they'll find out. Or you've disobeyed them, and you're afraid to tell what really happened. For some of you that front door might open to even deeper fears, more painful family situations. You're afraid of coming home to one more scene with a drunken mother or father. You're afraid there will be another fight between your parents, and you're wondering how long their marriage can last, and what will happen to you if they split up.

Or maybe you'd *like* to open your front door to a little noise. Your house is like a morgue—nobody there talks to anyone else. You each do your own thing and nobody seems to care about anyone else. You'd even like to have your dad chew you out sometimes for getting in late. At least then you'd know he was aware that you're around and was worried about you a little. You're afraid that no one in your home *really* loves you.

Some of you may be afraid for someone else—a brother, a sister, a good friend who is really messed up with alcohol or some other chemical, or who is too deeply involved in a sexual relationship or caught in a circle of really bad companions. You care, and it hurts to see someone you love wrecking his or her life, but you don't know what to do about it.

On the other hand, maybe you come from a wonderful family, and you fear not being good enough for them. Your mom and dad are terrific, but they expect so much of you. You always want to do and be the best for them. You can see they've got a lot riding on you, and the pressure to be number one all the time is getting to you. Your fear is that if you let up even a little you'll disappoint the people you love most in all the world.

And then there are fears that are built into being a teenager in today's society, like the fears associated with sexuality. Some of you may be getting in over your heads, into sex too soon, too casually, with the wrong person. You're afraid you might be losing something you'll never be able to recover, like self-respect. And some of you are afraid that you're not into the boy-girl thing *enough*. You're afraid that no one is ever going to notice you, that you'll never find a boyfriend or girlfriend of your very own. You fear there must be something wrong with you because you don't even know how to talk to members of the opposite sex.

Maybe your own disregard for other people's things scares you. You're in the habit of vandalizing or stealing, and you live in a kind of constant fear that you might get caught. Or, on a deeper level, when you really think about it, you're afraid of the kind of person you see yourself becoming.

Maybe it's the party scene that has you worried. You can't even remember much about last Friday's party, or the one before that. You find that it's getting harder and harder to say no to getting drunk or high. And maybe you fear the consequences that would come if you did say no. Would your friends drop you? And what would you do every Friday night if you weren't out partying?

And then there are those "megafears" that surround us in the world: cancer-causing chemicals in the foods we eat, contaminated and shrinking groundwater reservoirs, AIDS, big holes in the ozone layer, tornadoes and tidal waves, airplane crashes, nuclear war, and more.

What do we do in the face of all these fears? We whistle a lot, and pretend a lot, and laugh a lot, and try hard not to think about it all. And always we are deeply hoping that someone out there really loves us, and really cares about us, and *really* protects our little lives in this huge dangerous world we live in.

Where is God in all of this? God is right there, looking lovingly into the eyes of his frightened children and saying, "I care. I love you enough. Talk to me. I'll listen. I know how hard it is for you to be growing up in your world. You don't have to be afraid. I'm here, really I am! Tell me about your fears. Things aren't so scary when they're shared with me. You don't have to face them, any of them, alone. I'm always here. Don't be afraid."

2. When you finish your talk, play or sing with the group "Be Not Afraid." Next, allow a few minutes of reflective silence, then say:

When I finish giving these few directions, move quietly to your small-group cozy corners. Your group leader will take one of these lighted candles with you. When you get into your corner, sit on the floor in a tight circle. Then pass the candle around the circle twice. The first time you pass it, share one fear you brought to this retreat and one expectation or hope you have because you are here. The second time, pass the candle in silence. Hold it quietly for a few moments. Everyone in the circle is to pray silently for the person holding the candle. Pray to the God who lives in that person's heart for peace and courage, and for the special graces he or she needs and hopes to receive on this retreat.

When everyone has been prayed for, put the candle on the floor in the center of your group. Then reach out and touch the candle with one hand to symbolize our unity in Christ and his constant loving presence in our midst. Pray together the Our Father and Hail Mary, asking for protection from all the things we fear.

After your prayer, go *quietly* to bed.

The Web

(Reconciliation Prayer Experience)

This activity is a beautiful way to help young people become aware of the power of social sin in their lives. It can be used as a prayer experience in itself or as a preparation for the sacrament of reconciliation. It can also be used, at the discretion of the priest celebrant, as a communal penance service.

Materials and Preparations Needed:

▸ a skein of yarn wound into a tight ball. If your group is larger than 25, you will need two skeins.

▸ six candles in glass holders (the flame should be far down inside the glass)

▸ a large pair of sharp scissors

▸ chairs for all participants arranged in one large circle

Directions:

1. Ask everyone to move into the circle of chairs. If your group has been divided into permanent small groups, have them sit so that the members of each small group are together in the circle. (This helps to spread the adult leaders throughout the circle and to separate friends who might be disruptive during the serious part of the activity.)

2. The creating of the web is done playfully. Toss the ball of yarn across the circle, holding on to the loose end. (Send the first toss to someone who is likely to be serious about the sharing that is coming later.) Tell the receiver to pull the yarn taut, hold on to the end, and toss the ball to someone across the circle. Continue tossing back and forth until everyone is holding a piece of the web. (The new toss should always go cleanly across the top of the web. If someone misses a catch, have everyone help to straighten out the tangles before continuing.)

3. Ask the group to raise the web so that you can crawl under it with the lighted candles. Spread these out in a circle under the web. Crawl out (if the group will let you!) and turn out all the lights in the room.

4. Quiet the group and ask them to listen seriously as you explain the meaning of this web you have just created. Then present a talk based on the following script:

Script

The web we have made here tonight is a symbol of one of the basic truths about life—that we are social persons. Our lives touch and intermingle in hundreds of ways each day. Everything we do and say affects the people around us, and we are affected by the words and actions of all the persons whose lives touch ours.

This interaction of words, ideas, and actions creates a common energy field that is a constant influence on our attitudes, our values, our thoughts, and our decisions. We all contribute to that energy field and we all draw from it. It can be a power for good in our lives, but it can also be a power for evil.

Tonight we are going to focus on the negative aspects of the web—we're going to talk about *sin*. Every sinful choice we make affects the lives of those who share our world with us. For example: You come home from school and are deliberately unkind to your little brother; he punches your sister; your mom yells impatiently at all three of you; and soon the repercussions of your unkindness are reverberating through the whole family. Another example: You're sitting in the school cafeteria and you start making fun of a skinny freshman boy at the next table; your friends laugh and add a few more digs; and before you know it the poor freshman is the center of a whole group of upperclassmen "having fun" at his expense. I've seen kids get tangled in a web of meanness like this the first week of school and never really get out again.

What I want you to do tonight is think deeply about some of the ways you might be contributing to the web of sin in your world:

▸ gossiping about friends and classmates, starting rumors or passing them on;

▸ treating teachers disrespectfully, creating a negative, rebellious climate in the classroom and school;

▸ using parties as occasions of drunkenness and vandalism; encouraging by your tolerant attitude the misuse of alcohol, pot, and other drugs;

▸ urging your girlfriend or boyfriend to "go too far" sexually;

▸ treating sex casually, making jokes about it, bragging about it, thus adding to the climate of permissiveness in your group;

▸ being negative about going to Mass or religion classes, influencing the religious attitudes of your friends, and of the younger children in your family;

▸ lying to your parents, with one lie leading to another, until you and they are caught in a web of mistrust and suspicion;

▸ driving irresponsibly, or encouraging another driver to do so, thus endangering the lives of your friends and other people on the highway.

As you can see, sins like these are not just private matters between us and God. These are all public sins. We do them openly; sometimes we even brag about doing them. I'm going to invite you now to do something that may be very difficult for you. Because sin is public and affects everyone around us, we're going to publicly acknowledge our sin and ask God and our friends to forgive us. It will work like this: I'll begin by stating one of the ways I contribute to the web of sin in my world. I will then ask forgiveness of God and of you, my brothers and sisters. Then I'll tug on the yarn; the person at the other end of the tug will be next. That person will tell how he or she contributes to the web of sin, will ask forgiveness, and will then pass the tug on.

When it's your turn you can say something like: "I contribute to the web of sin in my world by gossiping about a certain teacher," or " . . . by lying to my parents," or " . . . by encouraging my friends to drink at parties." If you can't think of what to say when your turn comes, or you don't want to acknowledge a specific sin, just say something like: "I ask God to forgive me for all the ways I bring sin into my world."

Spend a few minutes now thinking about what you will say when it's your turn to speak.

5. Begin the acknowledgment process by saying, "I contribute to the web of sin in my world by _____, and I ask God and this group to forgive me." Then tug on the yarn.

   Note: Young people are usually very reverent during this activity. If, however, someone should begin to misbehave, stop the process and call for a respectful silence before continuing.

6. When the tug has gone all around the circle, say:

   One of the consoling truths of our Christian faith is that God loves us even in our sin. God's love waits patiently for a chance to forgive us and to help us overcome our sinful habits. In the eyes of God what we have just done is beautiful because by acknowledging our sin we have opened our hearts to God's grace and made it possible for him to untangle the web of sin in our hearts.

   As a sign of the power of God's forgiving love to cut through the webs of sin we leave, we will now cut the web.

7. Take the scissors and walk through the web, cutting every strand. (Be sure the cut ends don't fall into the vigil lights!) After cutting the web, close with this reading from Paul's letter to the Colossians:

   You must put to death, then, the earthly desires at work in you, such as sexual immorality, indecency, lust, evil passions, and greed (for greed is a form of idolatry). But now you must get rid of all these things: anger, passion, and hateful feelings. No insults or obscene talk must ever come from your lips. Do not lie to one another, for you have put off the old self with its habits and have put on the new self. This is the new being which God, its Creator, is constantly renewing in his own image, in order to bring you to a full knowledge of himself. You are the people of God; he loved you and chose you for his own good. So then, you must clothe yourselves with compassion, kindness, humility, gentleness, and patience. Be tolerant with one another and forgive one another whenever any of you has a complaint against someone else. You must forgive one another just as the Lord has forgiven you. And to all these qualities add love, which binds all things together in perfect unity. The peace that Christ gives is to guide you in the decisions you make; for it is to this peace that God has called you together in the one body (Col 3:5, 8-10, 12-15).

Option: If you have a priest present, have him be the one to cut through the web as a symbol of his role in the sacramental forgiveness of sin. He could also give the talk after the acknowledgements and read the closing scripture. Follow the web experience with sacramental reconciliation (see pages 124-126).

Reconciliation With Individual Confession

Materials and Preparations Needed:

▸ the services of several priest confessors, ideally at least one for every ten retreatants

▸ sufficient time in your schedule to prepare for the sacrament and to allow each person as much time as required for individual confession

▸ privacy for the individual confessions or conferences. Try to provide at least one confessional with a screen.

▸ meaningful activities to engage the entire group while individual confessions are taking place so that a prayerful atmosphere is maintained throughout.

▸ copies of the "Preparation for the Sacrament of Reconciliation" handout (page 127) for each participant

▸ a recording of reflective background music

Directions:

1. Begin with the participants in the large-group area. Share a brief talk introducing the sacrament of reconciliation based on the script below.

Script

One of the things that is unique about the Catholic church is the sacrament of reconciliation, also called penance or confession. Reconciliation is a sacramental celebration of God's loving mercy. It is an opportunity for us to bring our sick and wounded souls to Jesus so that his love can heal us.

Sin is a powerful factor in our lives. No matter how much we want to be good, we often find ourselves making choices that we know are not according to God's will for us. One sinful choice leads to another until we find that we are caught in a habitual pattern of sin from which we can't seem to escape. Lying to parents, cheating on homework, misuse of alcohol, sexual experimentation, shoplifting, use of foul language—such sinful habits as these seem to take over our lives, sapping our wills of the energy needed to change them.

We can't do it alone. We can't just decide today to change our sinful habits and be new people tomorrow. We can't, but God can. The power of God's grace has changed many lives, and can change each of ours if we are open to that possibility. God works in our lives in many ways. He speaks directly to our hearts, he touches us through the example of our family and friends, he influences us through the writings of scripture and other inspirational books, he teaches us through the leaders of our churches, and he prods us through painful and difficult life experiences. But one of his most powerful means of helping us to overcome our sinfulness is the sacrament of reconciliation. This sacrament is a face-to-face encounter with God, represented by his priest. As honestly and candidly as possible we open our hearts, acknowledging whatever is offensive to God and asking for forgiveness and for the grace of true repentance. And the priest, speaking in the name of God and as the representative of the church, declares our sins forgiven and tells us to go in peace.

Shortly you will have the opportunity to celebrate the sacrament of reconciliation. Some of you may be afraid of that prospect. I *strongly encourage you* to go tonight. Confession is one of the seven sacraments of your church and should not be disregarded.

2. Introduce the priest confessors. Ask them if they would be willing to answer a few questions for the group about confession. Then ask the questions below, giving each priest a chance to comment on them. Finally, open the floor for questions from the youth.

Questions

▸ Young people often ask me why they have to go to confession, why they can't just ask God in their hearts for forgiveness. Would you answer that question for them?

▸ Sometimes teenagers worry about talking to the priest about something embarrassing, especially sexual sins. Can you address that worry?

▸ If someone goes to confession to you, what happens the next time you meet that person? Do you remember his or her sins?

▸ Would you explain to the group about the seal of confession?

3. Now invite the participants to ask any questions they might have about confession.

4. Write on the board (or on a chart) an outline of the total time allotted for confessions (one to two hours). Say:

These are the things we'll be doing over the next two hours or so. You can do them in any order, just make sure you check the list so you don't forget anything.

A sample list follows. You can add or delete activities depending on your own circumstances. The goal is to keep everyone in a quiet, reflective mood for as long as the individual confessions will take.

1. Examination of Conscience
2. Individual Confession
3. Letter to God (see pp. 111-113)

4.   Letter from God (see pp. 111-113)

5.   One-on-one dialogue with an adult leader (see p. 78)

6.   One-one-one dialogue with a youth leader

7.   Mail Bags (see p. 57)

5.   Give out copies of the "Preparation for the Sacrament of Reconciliation" handout. Say:

The first thing you will do is prepare to receive the sacrament of reconciliation well. This paper will help you examine your conscience and tell you the steps to follow in going to confession. (*You may want to go through the steps briefly with the group.*)

6.   Tell where each priest will be located and explain the option of going to confession behind a screen or confessing face-to-face. Provide one "waiting chair" near each confession place, and some method of assuring that someone is always waiting to be next. Don't allow the others to line up at the waiting chair. It is difficult to keep the teenagers in the line from chatting and causing a distraction to the persons who are next in line for confession.

7.   Give directions for each of the other activities on the list.

8.   Move to the chapel or prayer room to begin the reconciliation service. It may take 90 minutes or more for everyone to go to confession and complete the other activities. Keep the process flowing smoothly and, as much as possible, maintain an atmosphere of prayerfulness throughout.

Preparation for the Sacrament of Reconciliation

1. Quiet your mind and heart and ask the Holy Spirit to be with you. Pray that God will help you to see your inner self as he sees you—with all your strengths and all your faults. Ask him to help you to be absolutely honest with yourself and with the priest.

2. Spend some time examining your conscience. Consider your actions and attitudes in each area of your life. Ask yourself, "Is this area of my life pleasing to God or not?"

Faith

daily prayer
attendance and participation at Mass
use of God's name
respect for sacred persons, places, things
religious education

Family

respectful, loving relationship with parents
concern for brothers and sisters
responsibility and helpfulness at home
truthfulness
forgiveness

School and Work

respect for teachers and peers
serious study habits
honesty on tests and assignments
response to criticism and correction

Fun

use of drugs and alcohol
respect for property—vandalism, stealing
responsible driving habits

respect for authority
choice of entertainment—movies, TV, books
respectful language
peer pressure

Sexuality and Relationships

truthfulness and honesty
respect and responsibility
sexual control, chastity

3. Approach the priest for confession. When you enter the confession area, he will welcome you in the name of Jesus and the church.

4. Make the sign of the cross with the priest. He may pray over you with a blessing like: "May God who has enlightened every heart help you to know your sins and to trust in his mercy." You reply: "Amen."

5. Confess your sins to the priest. Simply and directly talk to him about the areas of sinfulness in your life that need God's healing touch.

6. The priest will talk to you about your life, encourage you to be more faithful to God in the future, and help you decide what to do to make up for your sins—your penance.

7. The priest will ask you to make an act of contrition. You can pray aloud in your own words, telling God that you are sorry for your sins and that you want to love him better, or you can recite an Act of Contrition that you know.

8. The priest will extend his hands over your head and pray a prayer of absolution, for example: "God, the Father of mercies, through the death and resurrection of his son has reconciled the world to himself and sent the Holy Spirit among us for the forgiveness of sins; through the ministry of the Church may God give you pardon and peace, and I absolve you from your sins in the name of the Father, and of the Son, and of the Holy Spirit." You respond: "Amen."

9. The priest will wish you peace. Be sure to thank him as you leave.

10. Return to your place and spend some time quietly thanking God for his loving forgiveness. Don't forget to do your penance.

Celebrating Eucharist

The Eucharist can and should be a high point on a retreat. The atmosphere of caring and belonging that has been developed throughout the retreat should culminate naturally in the sacramental sharing at Mass.

Keep the retreat Mass informal and warm, yet prayerful and reverent. If possible gather in a comfortable space. Use a low table for the altar and arrange floor cushions in an informal semi-circle around it. Provide a chair for the presider.

Involve the young people in as many ways as possible in both the planning and the celebration of Eucharist. Schedule about 15 to 30 minutes for planning. Assign a small group to each of the tasks listed on the "Mass Preparation" handout (page 129).

Mass Preparation

1. **Setting**
   - Determine where the Mass will be celebrated and prepare the space: altar, seating, lighting, decorations, etc.
   - Set the altar table: linen, candles, crucifix
   - Decide how the gifts will be presented. Prepare whatever vestments the celebrant will need (check with him in advance). Arrange for eucharistic ministers.

2. **Music**
   - Select songs and acclamations that fit the theme of the retreat.
   - Form a small group to lead the singing.
   - Assign someone to introduce each song.
   - Choose recorded meditation music to be played during the reception of communion.
   - Give out and collect song books or papers.

3. **Readings**
   - Select readings that fit the theme of the retreat or use the readings for the day.
   - Choose readers and practice with them.

4. **Creed**
   - Prepare a creative way to present the creed with more than one reader or in song.

5. **Prayer of the Faithful**
   - Prepare five or six petitions that flow from the content of the retreat. Remember the needs of the world, of the church, of the poor and oppressed, of your own parish and family.
   - Choose a response for the petitions; for example, Lord, hear our prayer; or Hear us, O God.
   - Determine how you will present the petitions: one reader for all, different readers for each, or some other way.

6. **Communion Meditation**
   - Prepare and present a reflection experience to be used after Holy Communion. Some possibilities:
     - a reflective reading
     - a musical number, recorded or live
     - a litany of thanksgiving
     - a slide show
     - a simple liturgical dance
     - a faith-sharing activity, such as passing a candle or witness statements

GAMES

Squares of Fortune

This game is based on the popular TV game show "Wheel of Fortune." If you are not familiar with the game, it is recommended that you watch it as an aid to understanding the directions given below.

Materials and Preparations Needed:

▸ one pair of dice for the leader (The dice replace the TV show's wheel.)

▸ a chalkboard or chart for recording scores

▸ answer keys (pages 135-136) for several rounds of the game

▸ several blank puzzle charts (page 137) for each team

▸ a felt-tip pen for each team

Directions:

1. Write the name or number of each team on the board. Have each team select a representative and a recorder.

2. The leader takes up the answer key for the first puzzle. Each team recorder takes up one blank puzzle chart.

3. When a team is "up," it has the following options:

   a) The team members can roll the dice and ask for a consonant. If that consonant is found in the puzzle, they receive the points indicated on the bottom of the puzzle charts multiplied by the number of times the letter is found.

   b) They can ask to buy a vowel. If the vowel they ask for is present in the puzzle, they are charged 10 points for each time it appears.

   c) They can ask for the blank spaces in the puzzle. No points are earned or lost.

   Note: Unlike the TV show, a team has only one play each round (unless they roll double 4s which gives the team one extra play).

4. No matter which option the team chooses, the team that is up can attempt to solve the puzzle before passing the play to the next team. A correct solution earns a bonus of 50 points.

5. If a team rolls double 3s, it misses its turn altogether and may not attempt to solve the puzzle. If a team rolls double 6s (bankruptcy), it loses all the points, positive or negative, accumulated in the current puzzle. It does not lose points from past puzzles.

6. A team that rolls double 4s (extra turn) can choose two of the options (a, b, and c above), or it can take one of the options twice.

7. When one of the teams solves the puzzle correctly, the leader chooses a new puzzle from the answer key and begins again with the next team in line.

8. The scores for each puzzle are recorded separately, but the scores from past puzzles are also kept on the board. After all rounds are played, determine which team won the most puzzles, which team had the highest individual score, and which team had the highest total score.

Sample Play

The Team 1 representative confers with his team and decides to try for a consonant. He shakes the dice, rolls a number 7, and asks, "Is there a T?"

The leader responds, "There is a T in square 1 and square 17." (All team recorders write T's in these two squares.) The leader records 14 points (7 for each T) for Team 1. Unless Team 1 can solve the puzzle, the play passes to Team 2.

Team 2's rep confers with her team and says, "We would like to buy an "A."

The leader says: "There is an A in squares 12, 14, and 18." Since vowels *cost* 10 points each, the leader records minus 30 points for Team 2. If Team 2 cannot correctly solve the puzzle, the play passes to Team 3.

Team 3's rep says, "We would like to know the blank spaces." There is no need to roll the dice since no points are earned or deducted.

The leader responds, "The blank spaces are numbers 4, 9, and 20." No score is recorded. The play passes to Team 4.

Play continues until one of the teams correctly solves the puzzle.

Option: Each small group can play the game independently in the following way:

1. Divide each table group into two teams. Give each team a blank puzzle chart.

2. Give each group leader a pair of dice and several answer keys. Tables that can overhear each other will need different puzzles.

3. Proceed with the game above, with the small-group leader giving the clues and recording the answers.

Scoring Chart

Consonants: Dice count per letter   *Specials:*

Double 1s—10 points per letter   Double 3s—miss a turn

Double 2s—20 points per letter   Double 4s—extra turn

Double 5s—50 points per letter   Double 6s—bankruptcy

Vowels: Minus 10 points per letter   Solving the puzzle—50

Blank spaces: No points won or lost

Directions for Preparing the Answer Keys

Prepare an answer key for each puzzle given below by writing the phrase on the blank answer chart. Leave spaces between words. When you have used all of these puzzles, create your own, or have your teams create them for each other. (No line can be more than 10 squares long, including spaces.)

PARABLE OF THE GOOD SAMARITAN	WE RECALL THE LAST SUPPER	MOTHER TERESA OF CALCUTTA
PAUL'S LETTERS TO TIMOTHY	LOVE GOD AND YOUR NEIGHBOR	FORGIVE US OUR TRESPASSES
READ FROM THE BOOK OF GENESIS	JESUS AND THE TWELVE APOSTLES	ANOINTING OF THE SICK
SACRAMENT OF HOLY MATRIMONY	OLD AND NEW TESTAMENTS	THE PROPHET JEREMIAH
THE LORD IS MY SHEPHERD	JESUS OF NAZARETH	SAINT FRANCIS OF ASSISI
THOU SHALT NOT COMMIT ADULTERY	HONOR THY FATHER AND THY MOTHER	MATTHEW MARK LUKE AND JOHN
CELEBRATE THE HOLY EUCHARIST	MARY THE MOTHER OF JESUS	MAY YOU BE ALWAYS IN GOD'S LOVE
SEEK THE KINGDOM OF HEAVEN	GIFTS OF THE HOLY SPIRIT	OUR CHURCH HAS SEVEN SACRAMENTS
FAITH HOPE AND CHARITY	YOU ARE THE BODY OF CHRIST	THE ACTS OF THE APOSTLES
IT IS I DO NOT BE AFRAID	LET THE CHILDREN COME TO ME	PARABLE OF THE BURIED TREASURE

SQUARES OF FORTUNE ANSWER KEYS

Sample

H	O	N	O	R
T	H	Y		
F	A	T	H	E	R
A	N	D		
M	O	T	H	E	R

Puzzle 1 — 1–30

Puzzle 2 — 1–30

Puzzle 3 — 1–30

Puzzle 4 — 1–30

Puzzle 5 — 1–30

SCORING CHART

Consonants: Dice count per letter
Double 1s—10 points per letter
Double 2s—20 points per letter
Double 5s—50 points per letter

Vowels: Minus 10 points per letter
Blank spaces: No points won or lost

Specials:
Double 3s—miss a turn
Double 4s—extra turn
Double 6s—bankruptcy
Solving the puzzle—50 point bonus

SQUARES OF FORTUNE

1	2	3	4	5	6	7	8	9	10

11	12	13	14	15	16	17	18	19	20

21	22	23	24	25	26	27	28	29	30

SCORING CHART

Consonants: Dice count per letter
Double 1s—10 points per letter
Double 2s—20 points per letter
Double 5s—50 points per letter
Vowels: Minus 10 points per letter
Blank spaces: No points won or lost

Specials:
Double 3s—miss a turn
Double 4s—extra turn
Double 6s—bankruptcy
Solving the puzzle—50 point bonus

Team Charades

Materials and Preparations Needed:

▶ a set of 3 x 5 cards with one phrase—like those below—written on each card:

The cow jumping over the moon

Santa and his reindeer landing on a roof

The Packers kicking a winning field goal

Snow White naming the seven dwarfs

Contestant choosing final answer on Who Wants to be A Millionaire

The pope blessing the crowd at St. Peter's

A fisherman catching a 30-pound muskie

An Olympic champion receiving a gold medal

Jesus curing the man let down through the roof

The Japanese bombing Pearl Harbor

▶ blank 3 x 5 cards

▶ pencils

Directions:

1. Gather in the large-group setting. Divide the group into teams of about eight persons or use the small groups you have already established. Ask each team to sit together. Say:

In my hand I have a set of cards. On each card is a phrase like "John eating a giant banana split with a fork." Each team will pick one of the cards and will have three minutes to decide how to act out the phrases so that the rest of us can guess what the card says. You may use actions, sounds, and gestures, but you may not use words. Every member of your group should have a part in your presentation. The phrase must be guessed exactly.

2. Hold the cards face down, and ask the small groups to send up a representative to pick one. Allow about three minutes for the teams to decide how they will present their phrases.

3. Call the group back together and select one team to do the first presentation.

4. When all the teams have performed, give each group a 3 X 5 card and a pencil, and say:

Now I'm going to ask you to make up the next set of phrases. Each phrase should fit the pattern: "John eating a giant banana split with a fork." Someone must be doing something specific. Your group will make up a phrase for another group to act out. Be as creative as you can.

5. Allow a few minutes for the groups to think up ideas and write them on the cards. Check to make sure the phrases are being worded correctly, then say:

   Now pass your card to the group sitting at your left, and take three minutes to plan your presentation.

6. Call the group back together for the second round of performances. The group whose phrase is being acted, of course, does not help with the guessing.

7. Give out another set of cards, have the groups think up another phrase, and pass the cards to the group sitting at their right. The game can continue for any number of rounds.

   Option: On another occasion play the game using all biblical phrases, e.g., "Peter walking on the water toward Jesus" or "Jesus feeding five thousand with bread and fish."

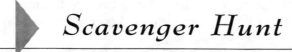

Scavenger Hunt

Materials and Preparations Needed:

▸ copies of the scavenger list (page 141)

Directions:

1. Give each team one or two copies of the list and say:

Your team must work together to obtain the items on this list. You have exactly thirty minutes. Please be respectful of the building and of other people's property; no points will be awarded for any item obtained through mischievous or destructive means. The decision of the judge, me, is to be accepted without question or argument.

Scavenger List

1. Three paper clips
2. The signature of the youngest person on the retreat
3. The signature of the oldest person on the retreat
4. A strand of red hair
5. A wild berry
6. Something purple
7. A Snicker's candy bar wrapper
8. A shoelace that is not white, brown, or black
9. A piece of litter from McDonald's
10. A contact lens case
11. A cash register receipt at least one month old
12. A tube of Crest toothpaste
13. A movie or sporting event ticket stub
14. An oak leaf
15. A shirt with 10 or more buttons on it
16. A coin dated before 1980
17. Five pictures of one person who is present here
18. A baby picture
19. One twig in the shape of a cross
20. A bottle cap
21. A blue paper cup
22. A child's toy
23. A belt that can be fastened around two people
24. A pair of red-striped pajamas
25. A show of gratitude for your wonderful retreat directors

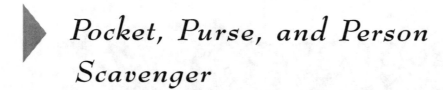

Pocket, Purse, and Person Scavenger

Directions:

1. Divide the group into even-numbered teams. If some groups are short one person, have them designate in advance someone who will always be counted twice.

2. Have the group decide on a team name. Record the names of the teams across the top of the chalkboard.

3. Call out items like those listed below. The items must already be present at the table—in pockets or purses or on the persons. Record the scores on the chalkboard.

4. Say:

    I will give your team one point for each button on your clothing. The button must have a corresponding buttonhole to be counted. (*Pause.*)

    The person with the holiest sock will win 25 points for his or her team. (*Pause.*)

    Fifty points for the team that can produce the oldest penny. (*Pause.*)

5. Continue with the following:

1	point for each belt loop
3	points for each stick of unchewed gum
5	points for each pair of non-jeans
25	points for the smallest shoe
25	points for the largest shoe
3	points for each lipstick or chapstick
25	points for the widest hand spread
2	points for each brother or sister (not counting yourself)
50	points for the longest single shoelace
5	points for each digital watch
5	points for each pair of glasses (not contacts)
10	points for each February birthday
25	points for the longest belt
5	points for each piece of religious jewelry
50	points for the longest strand of hair
1	point for each letter in everyone's last name
25	points for the oldest person present
1	point for each letter printed on a shirt; labels and buttons don't count

▶ *Teakettle Homonym Game*

Materials and Preparations Needed:

- ▶ a set of "teakettle" cards (see directions on page 144)

- ▶ some blank 3 x 5 cards

- ▶ pencils

- ▶ a chalkboard or chart for recording points

Directions:

1. Divide the large group into two teams. Say:

    Each of the cards in my hand contains a homonym, words like *hear/here* with the same sound but two different spellings and two different meanings. One team picks a card and makes up sentences that contain the homonym. However, instead of saying the homonym itself, the person giving a sentence says the word *teakettle*. The person can use either meaning of the homonym or both meanings in the sentence. The other team tries to guess what the homonym is.

    Some sentences for *hear/here* would be:

    It's so noisy in teakettle that I can't teakettle a thing you're saying.

    She wasn't teakettle yesterday so she didn't teakettle the announcements.

    Let's do one for practice. I'll give some sentences and you try to guess my homonym.

    Teakettle here, and I'll find out the correct teakettle.

    He had to teakettle in line to use the new teakettles in the gym.

    The longer I teakettle to start my diet, the worse my teakettle gets.

    Just in case you haven't guessed it, the homonym for the above sentences is wait/weight.

2. Ask someone from Team A to select one of the homonym cards and pass it around so that all the members of the team get to see it. Anyone who has a teakettle sentence can start. Each time the homonym is used one point is earned for the team.

3. Team A continues giving sentences until someone from Team B identifies the homonym. Team B then selects a homonym card. The play can continue for any number of rounds.

4. A team may wish to make up is own homonym rather than draw one from the pack. The homonym is then written on a blank 3 x 5 and passed around as above.

Directions for Preparing "Teakettle" Cards

1. Prepare 20 or more 3 x 5 cards. On each card print one pair of homonyms using a wide marking pen. Use the list on the next page and add any of your own.

2. Fold the cards in half so that the homonyms can easily be concealed from the opposing team when they are being passed around.

bored, board

bolder, boulder

ate, eight

meat, meet

ring, wring

see, sea

would, wood

fair, fare

principal, principle

flue, flew, flu

rain, reign

beat, beet

feat, feet

reel, real

wait, weight

plain, plane

pedals, peddles

peer, pier

piece, peace

right, write, rite

poll, pole

fourth, forth

flower, flour

pause, paws

chili, chilly

break, brake

new, knew

yolk, yoke

right, write

cite, site, sight

sail, sale

aisle, isle, I'll

beer, bier

steal, steel

toe, tow

doe, dough

our, hour

none, nun

morning, mourning

Puzzle Cards

Materials and Preparations Needed:

▶ a set of puzzle cards (pages 148-149). You may prefer to copy the puzzles onto large (6" x 8") cards.

▶ a sheet of paper for each group. Tell the groups to appoint a secretary who will number the paper from 1 to 40.

Directions:

1. Divide the cards into as many packs as you have groups. Put a pack of cards face down on each table. Say:

   On each of these cards you will find a number and a puzzle which stands for a common word or phrase. When I say "Go," turn the pack over, spread the cards out on your table and try to figure out the puzzles. When you know an answer, tell your secretary the number and the answer. Work quietly so you don't give your answers away to the other tables. When you finish the whole set, raise your hand.

2. When one group finishes, call "30 seconds." After the 30 seconds, say:

   Pack up your cards and pass them to the next table. (*Establish a pattern for rotating cards.*)

3. When all the groups have had all the cards, read the answers aloud. The table with the most correct answers wins.

Answers

1. paradise
2. backward glance
3. long underwear
4. see-through blouse
5. look around you
6. paradox or paramedics
7. reading between the lines
8. check up
9. mind over matter
10. touchdown
11. split level or bi-level
12. crossroads
13. Oh, gross!
14. neon light
15. high chair
16. downtown
17. sandbox
18. six feet underground
19. double date
20. I understand
21. tricycle
22. broken off or cut off
23. he's beside himself
24. side by side
25. man overboard
26. double cross or tea for two
27. Lucille Ball
28. black-and-white TV
29. split pea soup
30. son of a gun
31. little house on the prairie
32. equal rights
33. sleeping on the job
34. scrambled eggs
35. four degrees below zero
36. no room in the inn
37. search high and low
38. quarterback sack
39. three blind mice
40. Count Dracula

Puzzle Cards

DICE DICE **1**	DOCTOR DOCTOR **6**	LE VEL **11**	TOWN **16**
ECNALG **2**	R|E|A|D|I|N|G **7**	R ROAD OAD D **12**	SAND **17**
WEAR LONG **3**	K C E H C **8**	O-144 **13**	GROUND FEET FEET FEET FEET FEET FEET **18**
E C O D 78 **4**	MIND MATTER **9**	KNEE LIGHT **14**	DATE DATE **19**
L K YOU O O **5**	TOUCH **10**	CHAIR **15**	STAND I **20**

Puzzle Cards

CYCLE CYCLE CYCLE **21**	† † **26**	house PRAIRIE **31**	HOROOMTEL MOROOMTEL INN **36**
OFF **22**	E L U C L L I **27**	RIGHT= RIGHT **32**	SEARCH AND **37**
HE'S / HIMSELF **23**	**T.V.** **28**	SLEEPING JOB **33**	25¢ REFUND **38**
SIDE / SIDE **24**	SOUF? **29**	E G S G S E G G G E G S S G G E **34**	m ce m ce m ce **39**
MAN BOARD **25**	GUN, Jr. **30**	O / Ph.D M.D. M.A. L L.D. **35**	1. D 5 U 2. R 6 L 3. A 7. A 4. C **40**

Word Scramble

Materials and Preparations:

▸ Create a set of cards about 2" x 8", putting a scrambled word with number on each card (see examples below). There is an arrow on each word which indicates where the word begins. Do not tell your group this. Let the participants figure it out for themselves.

Directions:

1. Give each group a sheet of paper. Tell the groups to appoint a secretary who will number the paper from 1 to 25.

2. Divide the cards into as many packs as you have groups.

3. Put a pack of cards face down on each table. Say:

On each of these cards you will find a number and scrambled letters which can be recombined to form a common word. When I say "Go," turn the pack over, spread the cards out on your table and try to figure out the words. When you know an answer, tell your secretary the number and the answer. Work quietly so you don't give your answers away to the other tables. When you finish the whole set, raise your hand.

4. When one group finishes, call "30 seconds." After the 30 seconds, say:

Pack up your cards and pass them to the next table. (*Establish a pattern for rotating the cards.*)

5. When all the groups have had all the cards, read the answers aloud. The table with the most correct answers wins.

Sample Scrambled Words

1. HTACCOIL   CATHOLIC
2. TAFIH   FAITH
3. IIIINNTTAO   INITIATION
4. HCRTSIAEU   EUCHARIST
5. TAPBMSI   BAPTISM
6. TINNAOIGN   ANOINTING
7. YOHL RIITPS   HOLY SPIRIT
8. NICYTUMMO   COMMUNITY
9. TSCNAIIHR   CHRISTIAN
10. FANOOCNMRIIT   CONFIRMATION
11. TERUPCRIS   SCRIPTURE
12. PIBHOS   BISHOP
13. NIIYTTR   TRINITY
14. NAARICNNOTI   INCARNATION
15. CEEIOSD   DIOCESE
16. LOIIGRNE   RELIGION
17. RHHUCC   CHURCH
18. GULYRIT   LITURGY
19. SSUEJ SIHTCR   JESUS CHRIST
20. RYTOMILA   MORALITY
21. CCNNOOIIITALER RECONCILIATION
22. SSEEHPNIA   EPHESIANS
23. SNAIHTNIROC   CORINTHIANS
24. MTCCHIASE   CATECHISM
25. NVAEEH   HEAVEN

APPENDIX

Grouping Methods

Name tags If you know ahead of time who will be attending the session, you can use name tags to designate the groups.

- ▶ Before the session make a name tag for each participant, youth and adult.

- ▶ Put the name tags in groups of eight, determining the distribution you want in each group.

- ▶ Put a group symbol (number, letter, sign) on each name tag in each pack; put a corresponding symbol at each table.

- ▶ Make a list of the members of each group to give to the group leaders.

- ▶ Put all the name tags back in alphabetical order so they will be easy for the participants to pick up.

- ▶ As participants arrive, ask them to sit at the table marked with their symbol.

Friendship-group distribution This is my favorite method for establishing new groups at a retreat.

- ▶ As the participants arrive, invite them to sit at tables wherever they choose. They will sit with their friends.

- ▶ Give out small cards (or registration cards), one to each person. Have a different color card for boys, girls, and group leaders. Ask the participants to write their first and last name on the cards.

- ▶ Collect the cards yourself, being careful to keep together the cards of people who are sitting at one table.

- ▶ Decide how many groups you will need. If you need seven, for example, deal the cards into seven piles as follows: Begin with the group leaders, then distribute the cards of each group of friends. Try to balance the number of boys and girls in each group.

Playing cards This method works well for a short session with many participants, for example, a parent-youth evening.

- ▶ Arrange three decks of cards so that each suit is in order by number, ace through king.

- ▶ Decide how many groups you will need by dividing the expected attendance by eight. This will give you seven or eight in each group; for example, if you have a total attendance of 75, you will need 10 groups. For 10 groups, use only cards ace through ten in each suit.

▶ The way you give out the cards will assure the distribution of your participants. You will want each group to have some men, some women, some boys, some girls. Ask the men to stand and give them each a card in order—ace, 2, 3, 4, 5…. Then give a card to each woman, starting with whatever number is next in the pack. Next give cards to all the boys, then all the girls. Tell people not to take the same number as another member of their family.

▶ Put one card, ace through 10, in the center of each small-group circle.

▶ Have everyone move to the circle indicated by the number on his or her card.

▶ Ask someone in each group to collect the cards and bring them to you.

Count off This is the old stand-by for grouping. Its disadvantage is that some people will "forget" their number and move to a circle of their choice rather than to the one assigned.

▶ Decide how many groups you will need, for example, seven.

▶ Ask each person to count off, from one to seven. Count off the adults first, then the girls, then the boys.

▶ Move to the dialogue circles one group at a time: All the "ones" follow Mr. Jones, "twos" Mrs. Smith, and so forth. Moving one group at a time makes it more difficult for a person to "forget" and move to the wrong group.

Your-choice method Once in a while allow the young people to choose their own groups. Do this especially for shorter discussion activities of a personal nature. This works best when the groupings are just two or three people.

Retreat Rules & Regulations

(A Sample from the TYME OUT Center)

1. **Alcohol, drugs, and weapons** Retreatants showing evidence of having or using these substances will be sent home immediately.

2. **Dormitory restriction** Girls are never allowed in the boys' dorm or boys in the girls' dorm. Likewise, no one is to leave the dormitory after lights out. Anyone breaking these rules will be sent home.

3. **Safety devices** You will be fined and required to pay any damages for any tampering with fire extinguishers, fire alarm boxes, or smoke detectors.

4. **Meals** Because the various groups using the center eat together family style, it is important to be on time for meals. Each small group will be assigned to help with meal clean-up two or three times during the retreat.

5. **Dorms** The dorms are for sleeping only, not for lounging during the day. No food or drink is allowed in the dorms at any time. Pillow fights are not allowed.

6. **Off limits** Each group is restricted to the areas of the building assigned for its retreat. No one is allowed to leave the campus at any time.

7. **Doors** Please leave the building by assigned doors only. Outside doors and corridor doors should be kept closed at all times.

8. **Gym** The gym is for sensible play and fun, not for rough or destructive behavior. Gym shoes are required. No food or drink is allowed.

9. **Smoking** The retreat center is a smoke free facility.

10. **Cans** Please deposit all aluminum cans in the containers marked for them.

11. **Pillows and beanbags** The center is provided with many pillows and beanbags for your comfort. Please do not throw the pillows or jump on the beanbags.

12. **Damage** Please report any damage done to the building or property. Your group will be held financially responsible for the damage if it is evident that it is the result of rowdiness or vandalism.

13. **Consideration** We expect respect for and cooperation with the adult leaders who are giving their time to serve you on this retreat. We expect you to be respectful of the rights and needs of your brother and sister retreatants, especially their need for a good night's sleep. We expect respect for the other users and occupants of the building and for the neighbors, especially after 11:00 p.m. We expect respect for our building and property. Please be careful not to litter the outside grounds with candy wrappers and soda cans. Your group is expected to leave your retreat space as neat and clean as you found it.

▶ Notes to Group Leaders
(A Sample from the TYME OUT Center)

1. **Dialogue groups**

   Check registration cards for information regarding health, medicine, and diet. Please be responsible for monitoring these items for your group.

   Participate in the discussions at your table. Encourage the teenagers to share and to listen to each other. You yourself should try to listen more than talk.

   Direct your group in clean-up chores in the dining room and center.

2. **Overall discipline**

   Try to be where the teenagers are at all times.

   Sit among the teenagers in the dining room and meeting rooms.

   Watch especially for beanbag and pillow fights and other rowdy behavior.

3. **Dorm responsibilities**

   Position someone near each door.

   Don't allow pillow fights or other rowdy behavior. Collect any food.

   Don't allow teenagers to be in the corridor or to leave the dorm area.

   Put the lights out about 30 minutes after getting to the dorms, then require quiet.

4. **Morning**

   No one should get up before 7:30; everyone should be on time for breakfast at 8:30.

   Turn out all the lights before coming to breakfast.

   On the last morning, have everyone pack up before going to breakfast.

5. **Keys and change box**

   The leaders are given keys and a change box key. Your parish will be charged $25 for any key not returned.

   Please do not give keys to the teenagers.

   The gym must be locked when not supervised by an adult.

6. **Phone**

    Youth may use the phones only in the company of an adult.

7. **Fire**

    If a fire alarm sounds, lead the group out by the nearest exist and gather on the basketball court. Please familiarize yourself with the locations of all the fire extinguishers in the retreat area.

Printed in the United States
110638LV00003BA/7-124/P